WITH *Elisabeth Smith*

FAST GERMAN

HODDER
EDUCATION
AN HACHETTE UK COMPANY

For UK order enquiries: please contact
Bookpoint Ltd, 130 Milton Park, Abingdon, Oxon OX14 4SB.
Telephone: +44 (0) 1235 827720. Fax: +44 (0) 1235 400454.
Lines are open 09.00–17.00, Monday to Saturday, with a 24-hour
message answering service. Details about our titles and how to
order are available at www.teachyourself.com

For USA order enquiries: please contact McGraw-Hill Customer
Services, PO Box 545, Blacklick, OH 43004-0545, USA.
Telephone: 1-800-722-4726. Fax: 1-614-755-5645.

For Canada order enquiries: please contact McGraw-Hill
Ryerson Ltd, 300 Water St, Whitby, Ontario L1N 9B6, Canada.
Telephone: 905 430 5000. Fax: 905 430 5020.

Long renowned as the authoritative source for self-guided
learning – with more than 50 million copies sold worldwide –
the teach yourself series includes over 500 titles in the fields
of languages, crafts, hobbies, business, computing and education.

British Library Cataloguing in Publication Data: a catalogue record
for this title is available from the British Library.

Library of Congress Catalog Card Number: on file.

First published in UK 1998 as Teach Yourself Instant German
by Hodder Education, part of Hachette UK, 338 Euston Road,
London NW1 3BH.

First published in US 1998 as Teach Yourself Instant German by
The McGraw-Hill Companies, Inc.

This edition published 2011.

The teach yourself name is a registered trade mark of
Hodder Headline.

Typeset by MPS Limited, a Macmillan Company.

Printed in Great Britain for Hodder Education, an Hachette UK
Company, 338 Euston Road, London NW1 3BH, by CPI Cox &
Wyman, Reading, Berkshire RG1 8EX.

The publisher has used its best endeavours to ensure that the
URLs for external websites referred to in this book are correct and
active at the time of going to press. However, the publisher and
the author have no responsibility for the websites and can make
no guarantee that a site will remain live or that the content will
remain relevant, decent or appropriate.

Hachette UK's policy is to use papers that are natural, renewable
and recyclable products and made from wood grown in sustainable
forests. The logging and manufacturing processes are expected to
conform to the environmental regulations of the country of origin.

Impression number   10 9 8 7 6 5 4 3 2 1

Year   2014 2013 2012 2011

Contents

Read this first   vi
How this book works   viii
Progress chart   x

Week 1   Day-by-day guide   1
In the aeroplane • *Im Flugzeug* • New words •
Pronunciation • Good news grammar • Learn by heart •
Let's speak German • Let's speak more German • Let's speak
German – fast and fluently • Test your progress

Week 2   Day-by-day guide   17
In the Black Forest • *Im Schwarzwald* • New words •
Good news grammar • Learn by heart • Let's speak
German • Let's speak more German • Let's speak
German – fast and fluently • Test your progress

Week 3   Day-by-day guide   29
We're going shopping • *Wir gehen einkaufen* •
New words • Good news grammar • Learn by heart •
Spot the keys • Let's speak German • Let's speak more
German • Let's speak German – fast and fluently •
Test your progress

Week 4   Day-by-day guide   43
We're going to eat out • *Wir gehen essen* •
New words • Good news grammar • Learn by heart •
Say it simply • Let's speak German • Let's speak more
German • Let's speak German – fast and fluently • Spot the
keys • Test your progress • Well on the way

Week 5   Day-by-day guide   61
On the move • *Unterwegs* • New words • Good news
grammar • Learn by heart • Let's speak German •
Let's speak more German • Let's speak German – fast and
fluently • Spot the keys • Test your progress

Week 6   Day-by-day guide   77
In the airport • *Im Flughafen* • New words • Learn by heart •
Good news grammar • Say it simply • Spot the keys •
Let's speak German • Let's speak more German •
Let's speak German – fast and fluently • Test your progress

Answers   92
German–English dictionary   98
English–German dictionary   105
Flash cards   112
Certificate   147

Read this first

If, like me, you usually skip introductions, don't! Read on. You need to know how **Fast German with Elisabeth Smith** works and why. You'll want to know how you are going to speak German in just six weeks.

When I decided to write this series I first called it *Barebones*, because that's what you want: *no frills, no fuss, just the bare bones and go!* So in **Fast German with Elisabeth Smith** you'll find:

- Only 356 words to say, well ... nearly everything.
- No tricky grammar – just some useful tips.
- No time wasters such as 'the pen of my aunt...'.
- No phrase book phrases for bungee jumping from the Lorelei.
- No need to be perfect. Mistakes won't spoil your success.

I've put some 30 years of teaching experience into this course. I know how people learn. I also know how long they are motivated by a new project before the boredom sets in (a few weeks). And I am well aware how little time they can spare to study each day (about ½ hour). That's why you'll complete **Fast German with Elisabeth Smith** in six weeks and get away with 35 minutes a day.

Of course there is some learning to do, but I have tried to make it as much fun as possible. You'll meet Tom and Kate Walker on holiday in Germany. They do the kind of things you need to know about: shopping, eating out and getting about. They chat to the locals, ask a lot of questions and even understand the answers – most of the time! As you will note, Tom and Kate speak German all the time, even to each other. What paragons of virtue!

To get the most out of this course, there are only three things you really should do:

- Follow the **Day-by-day guide** as suggested. Please don't skip bits and short-change your success. Everything is there for a reason.

- If you are a complete beginner and have only bought the book, treat yourself to the recording as well. It will help you to speak faster and with confidence.
- Don't skip the next page (**How this book works**). It's essential for your success.

When you have filled in your **Certificate** at the end of the book and can speak **Fast German with Elisabeth Smith**, I would like to hear from you. Why not visit my website www.elisabeth-smith.co.uk, e-mail me at elisabeth.smith@hodder.co.uk, or write to me care of Hodder Education, 338 Euston Road, London, NW1 3BH?

And please join me on:

Facebook at www.facebook.com/elisabethsmithlanguages

Twitter at www.twitter.com/LanguagesESmith

How this book works

Fast German with Elisabeth Smith has been structured for your rapid success. This is how it works:

Day-by-day guide Stick to it. If you miss a day, add one.

Dialogues Follow Tom and Kate through Germany. The English of Weeks 1–3 is in 'German-speak' to get you tuned in. 'German-speak' is English imitating the expressions and word order of German: *I have in the September holiday*. You'll soon get a feel for the language.

New words Don't fight them, don't skip them – learn them! The **Flash cards** and the recording will help you. Get your friends or family to test you. Or take the **flash cards** with you when you are out and about.

Good news grammar After you read it you can forget half and still succeed. That's why it's good news.

Flash words and flash sentences Read about these building blocks in the **Flash card** section. Then use them! They'll reduce learning time by 50%.

Learn by heart Obligatory! Memorizing puts you on the fast track to speaking in full sentences. When you know all six pieces you'll be able to speak in German for six minutes without drawing breath.

Let's speak German You will be doing the talking – in German.

Let's speak more German – fast and fluently Optional extras for more speaking practice without pausing and stumbling.

Spot the keys Listen to rapid German and make sense of it. Find the key words among a seemingly unintelligible string of sentences and get the gist of what's being said – an essential skill.

Say it simply Learn how to use simple German to say what you want to say. Don't be shy.

Test your progress Mark your own test and be amazed by the result.

Answers This is where you'll find the answers to the exercises.

Dictionary Forgotten one of the new words? Look it up in the dictionary.

◀⅃⅃ This icon asks you to switch on the recording.

Pronunciation If you don't know about it and don't have the recording go straight to **Week 1 Pronunciation.** You need to know about pronunciation before you can start Week 1.

Progress chart Enter your score each week and monitor your progress. Are you going for very good or outstanding?

Certificate It's on the last page. In six weeks it will have your name on it.

Progress chart

At the end of each week record your test score on the progress chart below.

At the end of the course throw out your worst result – anybody can have a bad week – and add up your five best weekly scores. Divide the total by five to get your average score and overall course result. Write your result – *outstanding*, *excellent*, *very good* or *good* – on your **Certificate** at the end of the book.

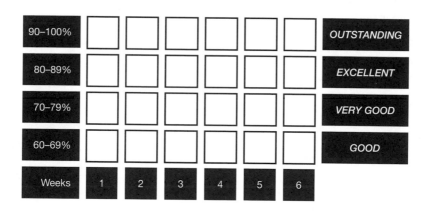

Total of five best weeks =

divided by five =

Your final result _____%

Week 1
Day-by-day guide

Study for 35 minutes – or a little longer if you can.

Day zero
- Open the book and read **Read this first**.
- Now read **How this book works**.

Day one
- Read **In the aeroplane**.
- Listen to/Read **Im Flugzeug**.
- Listen to/Read the **New words**, then learn some of them.

Day two
- Repeat **Im Flugzeug** and the **New words**.
- Listen to/Read **Pronunciation**.
- Learn more **New words**.
- Use the **Flash words** to help you.

Day three
- Learn all the **New words** until you know them well.
- Read and learn the **Good news grammar**.

Day four
- Cut out and learn the ten **Flash sentences**.
- Listen to/Read **Learn by heart**.

Day five
- Listen to/Read **Let's speak German**.
- Revise! Tomorrow you'll be testing your progress.

Day six
- Listen to/Read **Let's speak more German** (optional).
- Listen to/Read **Let's speak German – fast and fluently** (optional).
- Translate **Test your progress**.

Day seven – This is your day off.

In the aeroplane

Tom and Kate Walker are off to Germany. They board a plane to Stuttgart via Frankfurt and squeeze past a fellow passenger, who is sitting in their row.

Tom	Excuse me, we have seat 9a and 9b.
Klaus	Oh, yes, a moment please.
Tom	Hello. We are Tom and Kate Walker.
Klaus	Good day. My name is Becker.
Tom	Boris Becker?
Klaus	No, unfortunately not. I am Klaus Becker.
Tom	We are flying to Stuttgart. You also?
Klaus	No, I am flying to Frankfurt. But I am from Cologne.
Tom	I was in the May in Cologne. The town is very beautiful. I was for my firm in Cologne.
Klaus	What do you do?
Tom	Computers. I work at Unilever.
Klaus	And you, Mrs Walker? What do you do? Where do you work?
Kate	I was in a travel agency. I work now at Rover. The job is better.
Klaus	Are you from London?
Kate	No, we are from Manchester. We were three years in London and a year in New York. We are now in Birmingham.
Klaus	I was at Shell. I am now at the Deutsche Bank.
Tom	How is your job at the bank? Good?
Klaus	The job is boring. But there is more money. I have a big house, a Mercedes, a wife and four children. My wife is from America. She has parents in Los Angeles and a girlfriend in Florida and telephones always. That costs a lot of money.
Kate	We have now holiday. You, too?
Klaus	No, unfortunately not. I have in the September holiday. We are flying to Mallorca – but without the children. We have there a house – without telephone and without mobile!

2

Im Flugzeug

🔊 CD1, tr 2

Tom and Kate Walker are off to Germany. They board a plane to Stuttgart via Frankfurt and squeeze past a fellow passenger, who is sitting in their row.

Tom	Entschuldigen Sie, wir haben Platz neun a und neun b.
Klaus	O ja, einen Moment bitte.
Tom	Guten Tag. Wir sind Tom und Kate Walker.
Klaus	Guten Tag. Mein Name ist Becker.
Tom	Boris Becker?
Klaus	Nein, leider nicht. Ich bin Klaus Becker.
Tom	Wir fliegen nach Stuttgart. Sie auch?
Klaus	Nein, ich fliege nach Frankfurt. Aber ich bin aus Köln.
Tom	Ich war im Mai in Köln. Die Stadt ist sehr schön. Ich war für meine Firma in Köln.
Klaus	Was machen Sie?
Tom	Computer. Ich arbeite bei Unilever.
Klaus	Und Sie, Frau Walker? Was machen Sie? Wo arbeiten Sie?
Kate	Ich war in einem Reisebüro. Ich arbeite jetzt bei Rover. Der Job ist besser.
Klaus	Sind Sie aus London?
Kate	Nein, wir sind aus Manchester. Wir waren drei Jahre in London und ein Jahr in New York. Wir sind jetzt in Birmingham.
Klaus	Ich war bei Shell. Ich bin jetzt bei der Deutschen Bank.
Tom	Wie ist Ihr Job bei der Bank? Gut?
Klaus	Der Job ist langweilig. Aber es gibt mehr Geld. Ich habe ein grosses Haus, einen Mercedes, eine Frau und vier Kinder. Meine Frau ist aus Amerika. Sie hat Eltern in Los Angeles und eine Freundin in Florida und telefoniert immer. Das kostet viel Geld.
Kate	Wir haben jetzt Urlaub. Sie auch?
Klaus	Nein, leider nicht. Ich habe im September Urlaub. Wir fliegen nach Mallorca – aber ohne die Kinder. Wir haben da ein Haus – ohne Telefon und ohne Handy!

New words

🔊 CD1, tr 3

Learning vocabulary is always tedious. But you'll find that there are many English words which are similar to the German, so it's not that bad. Say these words out loud and don't worry because tomorrow you'll have **flash cards** to help you.

in/im in/in the
Flugzeug aeroplane
entschuldigen Sie excuse me
wir we
haben, habe/hat have/has
Platz place, seat
a... b (*pronounced* ah... bay)
und and
ja yes
ein, eine, einem, einen a
Moment moment
bitte please
guten Tag hello, good day
sind are
mein, meine my
Name name
ist is
nein no
leider unfortunately
nicht not
ich I
bin am
fliegen/fliege fly, are flying/
   am flying
nach to, after
Sie you (*polite*)
auch also
aber but
aus from, out of
war/waren was/were
Mai May
der, die, das, dem, den the
Stadt town, city
sehr very
4 **schön** beautiful, lovely, handsome

für for
Firma firm, company, office
was what
machen/mache make, do,
   are doing/am doing
arbeiten/arbeite work, are
   working/am working
bei at
Frau Mrs, woman, wife
wo where
Reisebüro travel office,
   travel agency
jetzt now
besser better
drei three
Jahr, Jahre year, years
wie how
Ihr, Ihre, Ihrem, Ihren your
gut good
langweilig boring
es gibt there is, there are
   (*lit.* it gives)
mehr more
Geld money
gross, grosse, grosses big
Haus house
vier four
Kinder children
sie she
Eltern parents
Freundin girlfriend
telefonieren/telefoniert
   telephone/telephones
immer always
das (by itself) that

das **kostet** that costs
viel much, a lot of
Urlaub holidays
ohne without

da there
Telefon telephone
Handy mobile phone

TOTAL NEW WORDS: 71
... only 285 words to go!

Some easy extras
These are all very similar to the English,

Die Mosnate (the months)

Januar	April	Juli	Oktober
Februar	Mai	August	November
März	Juni	September	Dezember

Zahlen (numbers)
null, eins, zwei, drei, vier, fünf, echs, sieben, acht, neun, zehn
  0   1   2   3   4   5   6   7   8   9   10

More greetings
hallo hello
guten Morgen good morning
guten Abend good evening
gute Nacht good night
auf Wiedersehen goodbye
tschüss bye

Pronunciation

🔊 CD1, tr 4

If German pronunciation is new to you, the recording will really help you. But if you are good at languages, or would like a refresher, here are the rules.

First the vowels

The English word in brackets gives you an example of the sound. Say the sound out loud and then say the German examples out loud. They can vary a little – sometimes the vowels seem a bit shorter and sometimes a little longer. That's why we've given you two examples for each sound. Don't worry – near enough is good enough.

a	(*star*/*cat*)	**ja, Tag, war, da, Name, haben/das, nach, hatte**
e	(*yes*/*name*)	**der, es, jetzt/dem**
i	(*in*/*feel*)	**in, ist, bin/Firma, wir**
o	(*no*/*pot*)	**gross, oder/kostet**
u	(*Peru*/*good*)	**gut, Juni, Juli/und**

Now the doubles

ai/ei	(*fly*)	**Mai, nein, drei, klein, langweilig**
ie	(*field*)	**Sie, wie, vier, telefoniert, viel, fliegen**
au	(*house*)	**Haus, Frau, auch, aus, August**

Now the consonants

j	(like *y* in *yes*)	**ja, Juni, Juli**
s	(like *z* in *zero*)	**Sie, sind, September**
v	(like *f* in *feel*)	**viel, vier**
w	(like *v* in *van*)	**was, wo, wie**
z	(like *ts* in *tsar*)	**zwei, Platz, Dezember**
sch	(like *sh* in *ship*)	**schön, Schiff (*ship*), entschuldigen Sie**
ch	(like the *ch* in *loch*), after **a**, **o** and **u**	**nach, noch, Kuchen**
ch	(like an exaggerated *h* in *Hugh*), after **e**, **i** and **ö**	**ich, schlecht, möchten**

The famous *Umlauts*

ä   (*care*)   **März, Mädchen**
ö   (*curve*)   **schön, zwölf, können** (*can*)
ü   This is a tricky one with no English equivalent. Try the way a Scotsman would say *noo* in *och aye the noo*. Then say: **fünf, Frühstück, Reisebüro**

And some more doubles

ee   (*say*)   **Tee, Kaffee**
eu/äu (*toy*)   **Euro, teuer, neu, neun, Verkäufer** (*sales assistant*)

Everything is pronounced in German: **Name** is not **'Nam'** but **'Na-me'**. Are you tearing your hair out? The recording will help you get it right.

Good news grammar

◀️ CD1, tr 5

This is the good news part of each lesson. Remember that promise: no confusing grammar? Every week I explain just a few things and talk you through the differences between English and German. This will help you to speak German easily.

1 Der, die, das

der, die, das, den, dem → all mean *the*
ein, eine, einen, einem → all mean *a*

Example   **der Platz, die Firma, das Geld, ein Haus, eine Frau**

So how do you know when to use which? Here's the first of the good news: In **Fast German with Elisabeth Smith** there is no need to struggle with what's what. You may muddle up your **der**, **die**, **das** but everyone will still understand you perfectly.

2 Saying 'you'

Germans usually use **Sie** (with a capital S) when talking to each other. This is a formal way of saying *you* and is always used – except to family, best friends and children, who are called **du**. When in Germany stick to **Sie**. It's much easier to use.

3 Doing things – remember to drop an 'n'

When you want to say *I fly*, **I do** or *I have* you drop the **n** from the end of the verb.

Example   **fliegen** → **ich fliege**
              machen → **ich mache**

4 Asking questions

Easy! You simply reverse the word order.

Example   You fly...   **Sie fliegen...**
              Do you fly...?   **Fliegen Sie...?**
              You have...   **Sie haben...**
              Do you have/have you?   **Haben Sie...?**

5 'There is', 'there are'

Use **es gibt** for both of these. You will use this a lot, especially when asking questions:

Example   **Gibt es hier eine Bank?**   *Is there a bank here?*
                Es gibt mehr Geld in   *There is more money*
                   Amerika.   *in America.*

6 Capital letters

All proper names and names of things (nouns) start with a capital letter in German: **Firma, Hans, Name, Geld, Kinder, Urlaub.**

Learn by heart

◀》 CD1, tr 6

Don't be tempted to skip this exercise because it reminds you of school… If you want to speak, not stumble, saying a few lines by heart does the trick. Learn **Mein Name ist…** by heart after you have filled in the gaps.

Example

Mein Name ist Amanda Hurley. *My name is Amanda Hurley.*
Ich bin aus Birmingham. *I am from Birmingham.*

When you know the seven lines by heart go over them again until you can say them out loud fluently and fairly fast. Can you beat 40 seconds? Excellent!

Mein Name ist…
Mein Name ist…
Ich bin aus…
Ich arbeite für eine grosse Firma.
Wir haben ein schönes Haus, aber es kostet viel Geld.
Ich war im Dezember in…
Wir fliegen im Juli nach…
Wie war Ihr Urlaub, gut oder langweilig?

Let's speak German

◀)) CD1, tr 7

Here are ten English sentences. Read each sentence and say it in German – out loud. You can check your answers on the recording.

1 My name is Walker.
2 Are you from London?
3 Yes, I am from London.
4 I have a girlfriend in Bonn.
5 We are flying to Stuttgart.
6 Do you have a Mercedes?
7 No, unfortunately not.
8 We have a house in Dresden.
9 There is more money in Köln.
10 How was your day, good?

Well, how many did you get right? If you are not happy, do it again.

Now here are some questions in German for you to answer in German. For the first five questions answer with **ja** and **ich** and for the last five questions use **nein** and **wir**.

11 Sind Sie aus Manchester?
12 Haben Sie ein Haus in London?
13 Fliegen Sie nach Frankfurt?
14 Arbeiten Sie ohne Computer?
15 Waren Sie für Ihre Firma in Bristol?
16 Fliegen Sie nach Berlin?
17 Haben Sie sechs Kinder?
18 Haben Sie im April Urlaub?
19 Waren Sie ein Jahr in New York?
20 Haben Sie jetzt mehr Geld?

Answers

1 Mein Name ist Walker.
2 Sind Sie aus London?
3 Ja, ich bin aus London.
4 Ich habe eine Freundin in Bonn.
5 Wir fliegen nach Stuttgart.
6 Haben Sie einen Mercedes?
7 Nein, leider nicht.
8 Wir haben ein Haus in Dresden.
9 Es gibt mehr Geld in Köln.
10 Wie war Ihr Tag, gut?
11 Ja, ich bin aus Manchester.
12 Ja, ich habe ein Haus in London.
13 Ja, ich fliege nach Frankfurt.
14 Ja, ich arbeite ohne Computer.
15 Ja, ich war für meine Firma in Bristol.
16 Nein, wir fliegen nicht nach Berlin.
17 Nein, wir haben nicht sechs Kinder.
18 Nein, wir haben nicht im April Urlaub.
19 Nein, wir waren nicht ein Jahr in New York.
20 Nein, wir haben jetzt nicht mehr Geld.

Well, what was your score? If you got them all right, you can give yourself a pat on the back.

Let's speak more German

🔊 CD1, tr 8

Here are some optional exercises. They may stretch the 35 minutes a day by an extra 15 minutes. But the extra practice will be worth it.

Don't worry if you don't get the **der, die, das** or the endings of some of the words right. This is about speaking – not about understanding complicated grammar.

In your own words

This exercise will teach you to express yourself freely. Use only the words you have learned so far.

Tell me in your own words that...

Example   *you are John Price*
           Mein Name ist John Price.

1 you originate from Manchester
2 you own a travel agency
3 you are a workaholic...
4 but you don't have a lot of cash
5 you have two children
6 your children are six and eight
7 your wife works for a company in Bath
8 your mother and father live in London
9 you have a vacation in April
10 you and your wife are off to America in December

Answers

1 Ich bin aus Manchester.
2 Ich habe ein Reisebüro.
3 Ich arbeite viel...
4 aber ich habe nicht viel Geld.
5 Ich habe zwei Kinder.
6 Meine Kinder sind sechs und acht.
7 Meine Frau arbeitet für eine Firma in Bath.
8 Ich habe Eltern in London.
9 Ich habe im April Urlaub.
10 Meine Frau und ich fliegen im Dezember nach Amerika.

Let's speak German – fast and fluently

◀)) CD1, tr 9

No more stuttering and stumbling. Get out the stopwatch and time yourself with this fluency practice.

Translate each section and check if it is correct, then cover up the answers and say the three or four sentences as quickly as you can. Try to say each section in less than 20 seconds. Some of the English is in 'German-speak' to help you.

Good evening, do you also fly to Hamburg?
Yes, I work there.
But now I have holiday.

Guten Abend, fliegen Sie auch nach Hamburg?
Ja, ich arbeite da.
Aber ich habe jetzt Urlaub.

What do you do in the holiday?
*I fly to Vienna (**Wien**) – for two months, June and July.*
The city is very beautiful.

Was machen Sie im Urlaub?
Ich fliege nach Wien – für zwei Monate, Juni und Juli.
Die Stadt ist sehr schön.

I have a girlfriend there.
She has a house.
A hotel costs a lot of money.
Oh, excuse me, please. One moment. There is my girlfriend.
Goodbye.

Ich habe da eine Freundin.
Sie hat ein Haus.
Ein Hotel kostet viel Geld.
Oh, entschuldigen Sie, bitte. Einen Moment. Da ist meine Freundin.
Auf Wiedersehen.

Now say all the sentences in German without stopping and starting. Try to do it in under one minute.

Test your progress

This is your only written exercise. You'll be amazed how easy it is!

Translate the 20 sentences without looking at the previous pages.

1 My name is Peter Smith.
2 Good day, we are Helen and Elke.
3 I am also from Hamburg.
4 I was in Frankfurt in October.
5 My wife and I were in America (for) three years.
6 We always fly to Berlin in June.
7 How was your holiday in England?
8 Excuse me please, what do you do now in London?
9 Are you Mrs Becker from Bonn?
10 The house in Hanover is for my children.
11 One moment please, I have the money.
12 Is there a telephone here? No, unfortunately not.
13 I am in England without my wife.
14 How big is your company?
15 Does a Mercedes cost a lot of money?
16 England is unfortunately not beautiful in February.
17 Udo has a girlfriend in the travel agency.
18 The day in Holland was boring.
19 My job is very good, but (a) holiday is better.
20 My two children have a lot of money.

When you have finished all 20 sentences look up the answers in the **Answers** section and compare them to yours. Then enter your result on the **Progress chart** at the front of the book. If your score is higher than 80% you have done really well.

Week 2

Day-by-day guide

Thirty-five minutes a day – but a little extra will speed up your progress.

Day one
- Read **In the Black Forest**.
- Listen to/Read **Im Schwarzwald**.
- Listen to/Read the **New words**. Learn 20 easy ones.

Day two
- Repeat **Im Schwarzwald** and the **New words**.
- Go over **Pronunciation**.
- Learn the harder **New words**.
- Use the **Flash words** to help you.

Day three
- Learn all the **New words** until you know them well.
- Read and learn the **Good news grammar**.

Day four
- Cut out and learn the ten **Flash sentences**.
- Listen to/Read **Learn by heart**.

Day five
- Listen to/Read **Let's speak German**.
- Go over **Learn by heart**.

Day six
- Listen to/Read **Let's speak more German** (optional).
- Listen to/Read **Let's speak German – fast and fluently** (optional).
- Translate **Test your progress**.

Day seven – **This is a study-free day.**

In the Black Forest

In Stuttgart, Tom and Kate hire a car and drive through the
Black Forest. They book into a hotel and then look for somewhere
to have a drink.

Kate Good day. Do you have a double room for one night and not
too expensive?

Hotelier Yes, we have a room with bath and shower. But the shower
is broken. My husband can that perhaps repair.

Tom Where is the room?

Hotelier It is here left. Is it big enough?

Kate The room is a little small and dark, but not bad. How much
is it?

Hotelier Only 40 euros for two, but no credit cards! There is breakfast
from eight to half past nine.

Tom Well... we would like the room. But can we the breakfast at a
quarter to eight have? We would like tomorrow at a quarter
past eight to Freiburg go.

Kate And I have a question: where can one coffee or tea drink?
Where is there here a café?

Hotelier There is a café five minutes from here, 30 metres right and
then always straight on.

(In the café...)

Waiter What would you like, please?

Kate We would like a cup coffee and a tea with milk.

Waiter Would you like also something to eat? We have apple cake.

Tom Two apple cakes, once with cream and once without,
please...

Tom My cake is terrible.

Kate But the cream is good.

Tom The table is too small.

Kate But the toilets are very clean.

Tom My tea is cold.

Kate But the waiter is handsome.

Tom The bill, please!

Waiter Nine euros 60 (cents).

Im Schwarzwald

◀》 CD1, tr 10

In Stuttgart, Tom and Kate hire a car and drive through the Black Forest. They book into a hotel and then look for somewhere to have a drink.

Kate   Guten Tag. Haben Sie ein Doppelzimmer für eine Nacht und nicht zu teuer?

Hotelier   Ja, wir haben ein Zimmer mit Bad und Dusche. Aber die Dusche ist kaputt. Mein Mann kann das vielleicht reparieren.

Tom   Wo ist das Zimmer?

Hotelier   Es ist hier links. Ist es gross genug?

Kate   Das Zimmer ist ein bisschen klein und dunkel, aber nicht schlecht. Wieviel kostet es?

Hotelier   Nur vierzig (40) Euro für zwei, aber keine Kreditkarten! Es gibt Frühstück von acht bis halb zehn.

Tom   Also... wir möchten das Zimmer. Aber können wir das Frühstück um viertel vor acht haben? Wir möchten morgen um viertel nach acht nach Freiburg fahren.

Kate   Und ich habe eine Frage: Wo kann man Kaffee oder Tee trinken? Wo gibt es hier ein Café?

Hotelier   Es gibt ein Café fünf Minuten von hier, dreissig Meter rechts und dann immer geradeaus.

(Im Café...)

Kellner   Was möchten Sie bitte?

Kate   Wir möchten eine Tasse Kaffee und einen Tee mit Milch.

Kellner   Möchten Sie auch etwas essen? Wir haben Apfelkuchen.

Tom   Zwei Apfelkuchen, einmal mit Sahne und einmal ohne, bitte...

Tom   Mein Kuchen ist schrecklich.

Kate   Aber die Sahne ist gut.

Tom   Der Tisch ist zu klein.

Kate   Aber die Toiletten sind sehr sauber.

Tom   Mein Tee ist kalt.

Kate   Aber der Kellner ist schön.

Tom   Die Rechnung, bitte!

Kellner   Neun Euro sechzig (Cent).

New words

◀)) CD1, tr 11

Doppelzimmer double room	**vor** before
Zimmer room	**viertel vor** quarter to
Nacht night	**morgen** tomorrow
zu too	**viertel nach** quarter past
teuer expensive	**fahren** drive/travel/go
mit with	**Frage** question
Bad bath	**man** one
Dusche shower	**Kaffee** coffee
kaputt broken	**oder** or
Mann man, husband	**Tee** tea
kann, können can	**trinken** drink
vielleicht perhaps	**Café** café
reparieren (to) repair	**Minuten** minutes
es it	**dreissig** thirty
hier here	**Meter** metre
links left	**rechts** right
genug enough	**dann** then
ein bisschen a little	**geradeaus** straight on
klein, kleine, kleines small	**Kellner** waiter
dunkel dark	**Tasse** cup
schlecht bad	**Milch** milk
wieviel how much/many	**etwas** some, something
nur only	**essen/gegessen**
vierzig forty	eat/eaten
kein, keine no	**Kuchen, Apfelkuchen** cake,
Kreditkarte credit card	apple cake
Frühstück breakfast	**einmal** once
von from	**Sahne** cream
bis until	**schrecklich** terrible
halb half	**Tisch** table
halb zehn half past NINE	**Toiletten** toilets
also... well...	**sauber** clean
möchten would like	**kalt** cold
um at (a certain time)	**Rechnung** bill
viertel quarter	**neun, sechzig** nine, sixty

TOTAL NEW WORDS: 68
... only 217 words to go!

Some easy extras

Zahlen *(numbers)*		Zeit *(time)*	
11	**elf**	**Uhr**	*clock*
12	**zwölf**	**um... Uhr**	*at... o'clock*
13	**dreizehn**	**um wieviel Uhr?**	*at what time?*
14	**vierzehn**	**eine Minute**	*a minute*
15	**fünfzehn**	**eine Stunde**	*an hour*
16	**sechzehn**	**ein Tag**	*a day*
17	**siebzehn**	**eine Woche**	*a week*
18	**achtzehn**	**ein Monat**	*a month*
19	**neunzehn**	**ein Jahr**	*a year*
20	**zwanzig**		
30	**dreissig**		
40	**vierzig**		
50	**fünfzig**		
60	**sechzig**		
70	**siebzig**		
80	**achtzig**		
90	**neunzig**		
100	**hundert**		
200	**zweihundert**		
300	**dreihundert**		
700	**siebenhundert**		
1,000	**tausend**		

Numbers up to 20 are very similar to the English. After 20 you say the number for the *unit* first:

24	**vierundzwanzig**
42	**zweiundvierzig**

Watch out for the time

halb zehn: think of it as half towards ten = *9.30*
halb vier = half towards four = *3.30*, **halb eins** = *12.30*

Good news grammar

◆») CD1, tr 12

1 Drop the 'n'

Remember to drop the **n** at the end of verbs when you say **ich**:

Essen becomes **ich esse**; **trinken** becomes **ich trinke**. Here's an odd one out: **können** becomes **ich kann**.

2 Splitting verbs

Germans like to keep you in suspense.

When they say: *We would like to eat Apfelstrudel with cream.*

They actually say: *We would like Apfelstrudel with cream...*
(to) eat.

Wir möchten Apfelstrudel mit Sahne...
essen.

So you don't know until the end what they are going to do to the cake – *buy* it, *bake* it, or perhaps *eat* it!

What happens is that, when there are two verbs in a sentence, such as **möchten** and **essen**, the second one gets put to the very end of the sentence. **Können wir ein Zimmer mit Bad... haben?** (*Could we have a room with (a) bath?*) **Ich möchte morgen in meinem Mercedes 600 nach Freiburg... fahren.** (*I would like to drive to Freiburg tomorrow in my Mercedes 600.*) If you forget and say: **Können wir haben ein Zimmer mit Bad?** there may be smiles all round, but everyone will understand you.

Learn by heart

◀》 CD1, tr 13

Learn the following seven lines by heart. Try to say them in under 50 seconds and with a bit of drama. Choose one of the following to fill in the gap: **meinem Mann; meiner Frau; meinem Freund** (*boy/male friend*); **meiner Freundin.**

Ich habe nicht viel Geld, aber...
Ich habe nicht viel Geld, aber ich möchte im Mai eine Woche Urlaub machen. Ich möchte mit _____ nach Frankfurt fliegen. Ich möchte von Frankfurt in einem grossen Mercedes nach Freiburg fahren. Ich möchte im Schwarzwald viel Bier trinken und Kuchen essen. Kann ich das machen? Ja, meine Firma hat ein gutes Reisebüro. Der Flug und eine Woche in der Pension Wolf sind nicht zu teuer. Es kostet nur 300 Euro.

Urlaub machen: *to make/have a holiday*; **Flug:** *flight*

Let's speak German

◀ CD1, tr 14

Over to you. I'll give you ten English sentences and you say them in German out loud. If you don't have the recording, check your answers against those printed opposite – but cover them so that you can see only one at a time.

1 We would like a double room.
2 It is unfortunately too expensive.
3 At what time is there breakfast?
4 The telephone is broken.
5 We would like to drink something.
6 Do you also have something to eat?
7 Where is the café, left or right?
8 The cup is not clean.
9 Can I please have the bill?
10 I am in London at nine o'clock tomorrow.

Now here are some questions in German. Use **ja** and **wir** for the ones on the left and **nein** and **ich** for those on the right.

11 Haben Sie eine Kreditkarte?
12 Möchten Sie nach Berlin fahren?
13 Haben Sie hier ein Telefon?
14 Möchten Sie um acht Uhr essen?
15 Können Sie morgen arbeiten?
16 Möchten Sie das Zimmer?

Now think up your own answers. Yours might be different from mine but still be correct.

17 Wo gibt es ein Café hier?
18 Um wieviel Uhr möchten Sie essen?

Answers

1 Wir möchten ein Doppelzimmer.
2 Es ist leider zu teuer.
3 Um wieviel Uhr gibt es Frühstück?
4 Das Telefon ist kaputt.
5 Wir möchten etwas trinken.
6 Haben Sie auch etwas zu essen?
7 Wo ist das Café, links oder rechts?
8 Die Tasse ist nicht sauber.
9 Kann ich bitte die Rechnung haben?
10 Ich bin morgen um neun Uhr in London.
11 Ja, wir haben eine Kreditkarte.
12 Ja, wir möchten nach Berlin fahren.
13 Ja, wir haben hier ein Telefon.
14 Nein, ich möchte nicht um acht Uhr essen.
15 Nein, ich kann nicht morgen arbeiten.
16 Nein, ich möchte das Zimmer nicht.
17 Es gibt ein Café *fünf Minuten* von hier.
18 Wir möchten um viertel nach *sieben essen*.

Well, did you get them all correct?

Let's speak more German

◀ CD1, tr 15

Here are some optional exercises. They may stretch the 35 minutes a day by an extra 15 minutes. But the extra practice will be worth it.

Don't worry if you don't get the **der, die, das** or the endings of some of the words right. This is about communicating – not about passing a test. Near enough is good enough.

In your own words

This exercise will teach you to express yourself freely. Use only the words you have learned so far.

Ask me in your own words...

1 if an en suite double room is available
2 what the price is for one night's stay
3 where you can have a coffee
4 if the café is straight ahead and on the left or on the right

Tell me in your own words that...

5 you would like breakfast at 7.30
6 you are thinking of driving to Salzburg the next day
7 you want tea and apple cake with cream

Tell me...

8 what you don't like about the café
9 what Kate likes about the café (**Sie sagt...** (*she says...*))
10 how much the bill is

Answers

1 Haben Sie ein Doppelzimmer mit Bad oder Dusche?
2 Wieviel kostet das Zimmer für eine Nacht?
3 Wo gibt es hier ein Café?
4 Ist das Café geradeaus und links oder rechts?
5 Ich möchte das Frühstück um halb acht.
6 Ich möchte morgen nach Salzburg fahren.
7 Ich möchte Tee und Apfelkuchen mit Sahne.
8 Der Tisch ist zu klein, der/mein Tee ist kalt, der/mein Kuchen ist schrecklich.
9 Sie sagt 'Die Sahne ist gut, die Toiletten sind sauber und der Kellner ist schön.'
10 Die Rechnung ist neun Euro sechzig.

Let's speak German – fast and fluently

◀) CD1, tr 16

No more stuttering and stumbling. Get out the stopwatch and time yourself with this fluency practice.

Translate each section and check if it is correct, then cover up the answers and say the three or four sentences fast.

Try to say each group of sentences in less than 20 seconds.

Some of the English is in 'German-speak' to help you.

Good evening, do you have a room with a bath?
Eighty euros is too expensive.
I would like a room with shower.
How much is (costs) the breakfast?

Guten Abend, haben Sie ein Zimmer mit Bad?
Achtzig Euro ist zu teuer.
Ich möchte ein Zimmer mit Dusche.
Wieviel kostet das Frühstück?

My company is here, 50 m straight ahead, on the left.
But I am going tomorrow to Hamburg.
I would like at 11.30 to go.

Meine Firma ist hier, fünfzig Meter geradeaus, links.
Aber ich fahre morgen nach Hamburg.
Ich möchte um halb zwölf fahren.

The café here is terrible and too expensive.
The toilets are not clean.
The coffee is cold and the cup is too small.
The bill? Eight euros for two apple cakes without cream?

Das Café hier ist schrecklich und zu teuer.
Die Toiletten sind nicht sauber.
Der Kaffee ist kalt und die Tasse ist zu klein.
Die Rechnung? Acht Euro für zwei Apfelkuchen ohne Sahne?

Now say all the sentences in German without stopping and starting. Can you do it in under one minute?

Test your progress

Translate these sentences into German and write them out.

See what you can remember without looking at the previous pages.

1 I drink a lot of beer.
2 How much is (costs) the breakfast, please?
3 Is there a travel agency here?
4 Do you have a table? In 15 minutes?
5 I would like to drink something.
6 My holiday in Florida was very good.
7 Where is there a good bed and breakfast place?
8 Can I have the bill for the telephone, please?
9 We were in Köln only once.
10 My children are big enough now.
11 At what time are you in the office tomorrow?
12 I am always there from half past seven to a quarter past five.
13 A question please: where are the toilets? Straight ahead?
14 We would lIke to fly to Oslo in January. But it is too cold.
15 Does that cost more money?
16 Where are you tomorrow at half past ten?
17 It is terrible, there is not one job without a computer.
18 Can we eat here now and do you have seats for six?
19 We have a small house in America, but it was very expensive.
20 Goodbye, we are going to Hamburg now.

Check your answers and work out your score. If it is above 70% you have done very well.

Now enter your result on the **Progress chart**.

Week 3

Day-by-day guide

Study for 35 minutes a day – but there are no penalties for doing more.

Day one

- Read **We're going shopping.**
- Listen to/Read **Wir gehen einkaufen**.
- Read the **New words**, then learn some of them.

Day two

- Repeat the story and the **New words**.
- Learn all the **New words**. Use the **Flash cards.**

Day three

- Test yourself on all the **New words** – boring, boring, but you are over halfway already!
- Learn **Good news grammar**.

Day four

- Cut out and learn ten **Flash sentences**.
- Listen to/Read **Learn by heart**.

Day five

- Listen to/Read **Spot the keys**.
- Listen to/Read **Let's speak German**.

Day six

- Have a quick look at the **New words**, Weeks 1–3.
- You now know 204 words. Well, more or less.
- Listen to/Read **Let's speak more German** (optional).
- Listen to/Read **Let's speak German – fast and fluently** (optional).
- Translate **Test your progress**.

Day seven

Enjoy your day off.

We're going shopping

Next stop Stuttgart and a week in a holiday apartment. Kate wants to go shopping but Tom is less keen.

Kate Well, we must today do the shopping. We are going with the bus into the centre.

Tom But the weather is bad. It is cold and there is a lot of sport in the television... Golf at half past twelve...

Kate I am sorry, but we must (go) first to a cashpoint machine at the bank and to the post office for stamps... and then to the chemist's and to the dry cleaner's.

Tom Well, no golf... perhaps football at three... Is that all?

Kate No, we must (go) also in a department store and a new suitcase buy and I must (go) to the supermarket and to the hairdresser's. And I would also like to (go) in a shoe shop.

Tom Oh, good grief! Until when are the shops open?

Kate I believe until six o'clock or eight.

Tom Ah well, also no football... perhaps tennis at half past eight...

(Later...)

Kate I think I have too much bought. 200 g ham, a piece cheese, a half kilo sauerkraut, a kilo potatoes, six Vienna sausages, bread, butter, eggs, sugar, four bottles beer and a bottle wine.

Tom No problem. That is enough for tomorrow. We have yesterday not much eaten. And what is in the big bag? Something for me?

Kate No, yes... Well, I was at Karstadt, at the hairdresser's and I have in a shop shoes seen, exactly my size. Are they not super – dark blue with white? The sales assistant was very nice and as handsome as Tom Cruise.

Tom Who is Tom Cruise? And how much cost the shoes?

Kate They were a little expensive. But they cost the same in England... 150 euros.

Tom What?... That is crazy!

Kate But this T-shirt for golf was very cheap, size 44, only 15 euros, wool with cotton, and here is an English newspaper... and is there not now tennis in the television?

Wir gehen einkaufen

🔊 CD1, tr 17

Next stop Stuttgart and a week in a holiday apartment. Kate wants to go shopping but Tom is less keen.

Kate Also, wir müssen heute einkaufen. Wir fahren mit dem Bus ins Zentrum.

Tom Aber das Wetter ist schlecht. Es ist kalt und es gibt viel Sport im Fernsehen... Golf um halb eins...

Kate Es tut mir Leid, aber wir müssen zuerst zu einem Geldautomaten bei der Bank und zur Post für Briefmarken... und dann zur Apotheke und zur Reinigung.

Tom Also kein Golf... vielleicht Fussball um drei... Ist das alles?

Kate Nein, wir müssen auch in ein Kaufhaus und einen neuen Koffer kaufen und ich muss zum Supermarkt und zum Friseur. Und ich möchte auch in ein Schuhgeschäft.

Tom Ach, du meine Güte! Bis wann sind die Geschäfte offen?

Kate Ich glaube bis sechs Uhr, oder acht.

Tom Ach, also auch kein Fussball... vielleicht Tennis um halb neun...

(Später...)

Kate Ich glaube, ich habe zuviel gekauft: 200 Gramm Schinken, ein Stück Käse, ein halbes Kilo Sauerkraut, ein Kilo Kartoffeln, sechs Wiener, Brot, Butter, Eier, Zucker, vier Flaschen Bier und eine Flasche Wein.

Tom Kein Problem. Das ist genug für morgen. Wir haben gestern nicht viel gegessen. Und was ist in der grossen Tüte? Etwas für mich?

Kate Nein, ja... Also ich war bei Karstadt beim Friseur und ich habe in einem Geschäft Schuhe gesehen, genau meine Grösse. Sind sie nicht super – dunkelblau mit weiss? Der Verkäufer war sehr nett und so schön wie Tom Cruise.

Tom Wer ist Tom Cruise? Und wieviel kosten die Schuhe?

Kate Sie waren ein bisschen teuer. Aber sie kosten dasselbe in England... 150 Euro.

Tom Was?... Das ist verrückt!

Kate Aber dieses T-Shirt für Golf war sehr billig, Grösse 44, nur 15 Euro, Wolle mit Baumwolle, und hier ist eine englische Zeitung... und gibt es nicht jetzt Tennis im Fernsehen?

New words
🔊 CD1, tr 18

gehen go
einkaufen to do the shopping
müssen/Ich muss must/I must
heute today
Bus bus
Zentrum centre
Wetter weather
Fernsehen television
es tut mir Leid I'm sorry
zuerst first
zu/zum, zur to/to the
Geldautomat cashpoint machine
Post post office
Briefmarken stamps
Apotheke chemist's
Reinigung dry cleaner's
Fussball football
alle/alles all
Kaufhaus department store
neu new
Koffer suitcase
kaufen/gekauft buy/bought
Friseur hairdresser's
Schuhgeschäft shoe shop
Geschäft, Geschäfte shop, shops
ach, du meine Güte! good grief!
wann when
offen open
glauben/ich glaube believe, think/
  I believe, I think
später later
zuviel too much
Gramm gram
Schinken ham

Stück piece
Käse cheese
Kartoffeln potatoes
Wiener Vienna sausages
  (hot dogs)
Brot bread
Butter butter
Ei, Eier egg, eggs
Zucker sugar
Flasche, Flaschen bottle, bottles
Bier beer
Wein wine
kein Problem no problem
gestern yesterday
Karstadt a well-known chain of
  department stores
Tüte bag (paper or plastic)
mich me
sehen/gesehen see/seen
genau exactly
Grösse size
blau blue
weiss white
Verkäufer sales assistant
nett nice
so... wie as... as
wer who
dasselbe the same
verrückt crazy
dies, dieser, diese, dieses this
billig cheap
Wolle wool
Baumwolle cotton
Zeitung newspaper

> **TOTAL NEW WORDS: 65**
> **... only 152 words to go!**

Good news grammar

🔊 CD1, tr 19

1 Remember: möchten, können, müssen

When these verbs appear, any second verb will move to the end of the sentence.

Example   Wir **müssen** heute viel Bier... **kaufen.**
We must today a lot of beer... buy. =
We must buy a lot of beer today.

2 Good news: shortcut!

Whenever you *would like to* or *must GO* somewhere you can drop the word *go*. But it's optional.

Example   Wir **müssen** zur Bank (gehen).
Ich **möchte** zu Karstadt (gehen).

3 Not so bad: the past

Imagine that you were getting married today. You would say: *I do.*
If it happened yesterday you would say *I did* or *I have done it.*

When you talk about something that happened before, or in the past, in German you use **haben** plus the other verb, slightly changed and often starting with **ge-**.

Example   **wir haben gekauft** *we have bought* or *we bought*

As in the case of **möchten, können** and **müssen,** when you use **haben** the other verb always goes right to the end of the sentence.

Example   *I have seen Tom Cruise.* Ich **habe** Tom Cruise **gesehen.**
We bought a car yesterday. Wir **haben** gestern ein Auto **gekauft.**

As you can see: another suspense story! Nobody knows right up to the end what we did to the car yesterday... *sold* it? *smashed* it up?

33

Once you get into the habit of putting the second verb at the end you'll have mastered half of **Fast German with Elisabeth Smith** grammar.

In the **Good news grammar** section of Week 6 there's a summary of all the verbs and verb forms. Whenever you get in a muddle have a quick look there.

4 Some easy extras – *Farben* (colours)

As a reward for the mental acrobatics with verbs, here are ten useful words for when you want to change that pink shirt for a green one...

weiss	**schwarz**	**rot**	**blau**	**gelb**	**grün**	**orange**	**rosa**	**grau**	**braun**
white	*black*	*red*	*blue*	*yellow*	*green*	*orange*	*pink*	*grey*	*brown*

Learn by heart

🔊 CD1, tr 20

Try to say these eight lines in less than one minute.

Wir müssen heute einkaufen

Wir müssen heute einkaufen – kein Problem!

Aber wo gibt es einen Bus zu den Geschäften?

Ach, du meine Güte! Ich glaube, ich habe nicht genug Geld.

Es tut mir Leid, aber wir müssen zuerst zu einem Geldautomaten.

Wir haben im Supermarkt viel gekauft: Brot, Butter, Schinken und Käse und zwei Flaschen Wein.

Es war nicht billig: fünfundzwanzig Euro, aber der Verkäufer war sehr nett.

The more expression you use when saying it, the easier it will be to remember all the useful bits.

Spot the keys

◀ CD1, tr 21

By now you can say many things in German. But what happens if you ask a question and do not understand the answer – especially if it hits you at the speed of a machine gun? The smart way is not to panic, but to listen only for the words you know. Any familiar words that you pick up will provide you with **Key words** – clues to what the other person is saying.

If you have the recording, close the book now and listen to the dialogue. Here's an example:

YOU   **Entschuldigen Sie bitte, wo ist die Post?**
ANSWER *Also, dasistganzeinfach.* **Erstmal immer geradeaus bis** *zurnächsten Kreuzung, dabeidem* **grossen roten Haus. Dann links,** *daistein Altersheimundmehrere* **Geschäfte.** *Undgleichdahinter* **rechts** *kommen Siezudem Park* **Platz** *vorder* **Post.**

Although most words run into each other when spoken you should have still managed to pick up:

immer geradeaus – bis – gross – rot – Haus – dann links – Geschäfte – rechts – Platz – Post... so you should be able to get to the post office!

Let's speak German

Now let's practise again what you have learned. If you have the recording, use it to check your answers. Read the sentences out loud, one at a time, then translate or answer them out loud.

1 I am now going to the post office.
2 When are the shops open?
3 I am sorry, but that is too expensive.
4 Where is there a bus to the centre?
5 We ate at Karstadt.
6 Can one buy wine in the supermarket?
7 Shopping without money? No, but with a credit card.
8 I bought everything in the department store.
9 Have you seen the weather on the TV?
10 Good grief, the suitcase is broken!

Answer the following in German using the words in brackets:

11 Haben Sie die Schuhe in Grösse 38? (ja, wir)
12 Haben Sie das Bier im Supermarkt gekauft? (ja, wir)
13 Haben Sie meine Frau gesehen? (nein, wir)
14 Müssen Sie um neun Uhr gehen? (nein, wir)
15 Haben Sie zuviel gegessen? (nein, wir)
16 Was haben Sie gekauft: ein Stück Käse oder Schinken? (Schinken)
17 Wer hat gestern billig gegessen? (ich)
18 Bis wann sind die Geschäfte offen? (acht Uhr)
19 Möchten Sie ein viertel oder ein halbes Kilo Kaffee? (ein halbes)
20 Gibt es einen Bus zum Hotel? (ja)

Answers

1 Ich gehe jetzt zur Post.
2 Wann sind die Geschäfte offen?
3 Es tut mir Leid, aber das ist zu teuer.
4 Wo gibt es einen Bus zum Zentrum?
5 Wir haben bei Karstadt gegessen.
6 Kann man im Supermarkt Wein kaufen?
7 Einkaufen ohne Geld? Nein, aber mit einer Kreditkarte.
8 Ich habe alles im Kaufhaus gekauft.
9 Haben Sie das Wetter im Fernsehen gesehen?
10 Ach, du meine Güte, der Koffer ist kaputt!
11 Ja, wir haben die Schuhe in Grösse 38.
12 Ja, wir haben das Bier im Supermarkt gekauft.
13 Nein, wir haben Ihre Frau nicht gesehen.
14 Nein, wir müssen nicht um neun Uhr gehen.
15 Nein, wir haben nicht zuviel gegessen.
16 Ich habe/Wir haben Schinken gekauft.
17 Ich habe gestern billig gegessen.
18 Die Geschäfte sind bis acht Uhr offen.
19 Ich möchte/Wir möchten ein halbes Kilo Kaffee.
20 Ja, es gibt einen Bus zum Hotel.

Let's speak more German

◀) CD2, tr 2

For these optional exercises add an extra 15 minutes to your daily schedule. And don't worry about getting the endings wrong. Near enough is good enough.

In your own words

This exercise will teach you to express yourself freely. Use only the words you have learned so far.

Tell me in your own words that...

1 you would like to do the shopping today
2 you are catching the bus
3 you are out of cash
4 you have to go first to a cashpoint machine
5 then you have to go to the pharmacy
6 you have to go also to a department store
7 you would like to buy shoes
8 you bought shoes, and they weren't cheap
9 you did not buy much in the supermarket
10 you bought bread and butter and a little beer – 12 bottles...

Answers

1 Ich möchte heute einkaufen.
2 Ich fahre mit dem Bus.
3 Ich habe kein Geld.*
4 Ich muss zuerst zu einem Geldautomaten.
5 Ich muss dann zur Apotheke.
6 Ich muss auch zu einem Warenhaus.
7 Ich möchte Schuhe kaufen.
8 Ich habe Schuhe gekauft und sie waren nicht billig.
9 Ich habe nicht viel im Supermarkt gekauft.
10 Ich habe Brot und Butter gekauft, und ein bisschen Bier – zwölf Flaschen…

* strictly speaking, *cash* is **Bargeld**

Let's speak German – fast and fluently

🔊 CD2, tr 3

Translate each section and check if it is correct, then cover up the answers and say the three or four sentences fast.

Try to say each group of sentences in under 20 seconds.

Some of the English is in 'German-speak' to help you.

Excuse me, are you going also with the bus?
Is this the bus for the centre?
Yes, there are two, Bus 7 and 19.

Entschuldigen Sie, fahren Sie auch mit dem Bus?
Ist dies der Bus für das Zentrum?
Ja, es gibt zwei, Bus sieben und neunzehn.

I would like a suitcase to buy, but not too expensive.
We have a suitcase, but it (he*) is too small.
I have a suitcase seen and it is big enough.

Ich möchte einen Koffer kaufen, aber nicht zu teuer.
Wir haben einen Koffer, aber er ist zu klein.
Ich habe einen Koffer gesehen und er ist gross genug.

* If you talk about something that is der, e.g. der Koffer, you say er (he).

The weather today was very bad. We were in Munich.
We have eaten in the Hofbräuhaus.**
Ham, cheese and potatoes – for ten euros.
The waiter wasn't handsome but very nice.

Das Wetter war heute sehr schlecht. Wir waren in München.
Wir haben im Hofbräuhaus gegessen.
Schinken, Käse und Kartoffeln – für zehn Euro.
Der Kellner war nicht schön, aber sehr nett.

** famous Munich beer garden

Now say all the sentences in German without stopping and starting.

Try to do it in under one minute. If you're not happy with your result, try it again.

Test your progress

Translate these sentences into German, in writing. Before you mark your work check again on the scoring instructions. Enter the result on the **Progress chart** and be amazed. You are now halfway home and it will be getting easier all the time.

1 Can you see a sales assistant?
2 Where can we buy something to eat?
3 When must you (go) to the office today? At seven? How terrible!
4 We saw that yesterday on (in the) television.
5 I believe the shops are now open.
6 Is there a department store here or a centre with shops?
7 Excuse me, are you also going to the post office?
8 Where did you buy the English newspaper?
9 Who would like wine and who would like to drink beer?
10 The weather will be (is) bad tomorrow. That is not nice.
11 That is all? That was cheap.
12 The stamps cost exactly five euros.
13 The cashpoint machine is for all credit cards.
14 Are 300 grams (of) cheese too much? No, no problem.
15 There is a new dry cleaner's three minutes from here.
16 Do you have a bag for my shoes, please?
17 I believe I have seen a chemist's here.
18 Good grief, all (the) eggs and three bottles are broken!
19 Can you see that? Is that cotton?
20 Size 12 in England – what is that here?

Check your answers and don't forget the **Progress chart**.

Week 4

Day-by-day guide

Study 35 minutes a day but if you are keen and manage to find the time, try 40… 45…

Day one
- Read **We're going to eat out.**
- Listen to/Read **Wir gehen essen**.
- Read the **New words**. Learn the easy ones.

Day two
- Repeat the dialogue. Learn the harder **New words**.
- Cut out the **Flash words** to help you.

Day three
- Learn all the **New words** until you know them well.
- Read and learn the **Good news grammar**.

Day four
- Cut out and learn the ten **Flash sentences**.
- Listen to/Read **Learn by heart**.

Day five
- Read **Say it simply**.
- Listen to/Read **Let's speak German**.

Day six
- Listen to/Read **Spot the keys**.
- Listen to/Read **Let's speak more German** (optional).
- Listen to/Read **Let's speak German – fast and fluently** (optional).
- Translate **Test your progress**.

Day seven
Are you keeping your scores above 60%? In that case, have a good day off.

We're going to eat out

Tom and Kate are off to dinner with an important client. But will Kate be able to handle the infamous Edith?

No more 'German- speak'. As you'll have realized by now not everything can be translated word for word from one language to the other. If you simply exchange the words, people may understand you and might even be amused, but saying things the German way will sound much better and will impress the locals.

Kate	Tom, someone telephoned. He did not say why. The number is on the paper by the telephone book. A Mr Schmidt from Frankfurt.
Tom	Oh yes, Horst Schmidt, a good client of the company. I know him well. He is very nice. I have an appointment with him on Thursday. That is an important matter.
Tom	*(On the phone)* Hello, good morning, Herr Schmidt. Tom Walker here… Yes, thank you… Yes, sure, that is possible… next week… of course… yes, very interesting… no, we have time… wonderful… no, only a few days… I see… when?… at eight o'clock… at the top by the exit, by the door. Well, until Tuesday, thank you very much, goodbye.
Kate	What are we doing on Tuesday?
Tom	We are going to eat with Herr Schmidt. In the centre, behind the church. He says the restaurant is new but cosy. Herr Schmidt is in Stuttgart for two days, with Edith and Peter Palmer from our office.
Kate	I know Edith Palmer. She is boring and knows everything better. She has a terrible dog. I think I am going to be sick on Tuesday. A heavy cold and pains. The doctor must come…
Tom	No, please, that's not on, one cannot do that.

Wir gehen essen

4)) CD2, tr 4

Tom and Kate are off to dinner with an important client. But will
Kate be able to handle the infamous Edith?

Kate Tom, jemand hat telefoniert. Er hat nicht gesagt, warum.
Die Nummer ist auf dem Papier beim Telefonbuch. Ein Herr
Schmidt aus Frankfurt.

Tom Oh, ja, Horst Schmidt, ein guter Kunde von der Firma. Ich
kenne ihn gut. Er ist sehr nett. Ich habe Donnerstag einen
Termin mit ihm. Das ist eine wichtige Sache.

Tom *(Telefoniert)* Hallo? Guten Morgen, Herr Schmidt. Tom Walker
hier... Ja, danke... Ja, sicher, das ist möglich... nächste
Woche... natürlich... ja, sehr interessant... nein, wir haben
Zeit... wunderbar... nein, nur ein paar Tage... ach so...
wann?... um acht Uhr... oben am Ausgang, an der Tür... Also
bis Dienstag, vielen Dank, auf Wiedersehen.

Kate Was machen wir Dienstag?

Tom Wir gehen mit Herrn Schmidt essen. Im Zentrum, hinter der
Kirche. Er sagt, das Restaurant ist neu aber gemütlich. Herr
Schmidt ist für zwei Tage in Stuttgart, mit Edith und Peter
Palmer von unserer Firma.

Kate Ich kenne Edith Palmer. Sie ist langweilig und weiss alles
besser. Sie hat einen schrecklichen Hund. Ich glaube, ich bin
am Dienstag krank. Eine schwere Erkältung und Schmerzen.
Der Arzt muss kommen.

Tom Nein, bitte, das geht nicht, das kann man nicht machen!

(In the restaurant...)

Waiter   The fish is not on the menu and the dessert today is Apfelstrudel with ice cream or cream.

Horst   Mrs Walker, can I help you? Perhaps a soup… and then afterwards?

Kate   I would very much like the steak with salad, please.

Edith   I think too much red meat is not good for you, Kate.

Horst   Mr Walker, what can we give you? And what would you like to drink? Wine?

Tom   I would prefer a beer and then the fried sausage, with potatoes and vegetables, please.

Edith   Tom, the vegetables are in cream. I would not like to eat that.

Horst   And you, Mrs Palmer?

Edith   A little chicken from the grill, fruit and a glass of water, please.

(Later…)

Horst   Are we all ready? It is late. Would anybody like a cup of coffee? Nobody? Good, the bill please.

Edith   Oh, Herr Schmidt, can you help me please!
How do you say 'doggy bag' in German?
I would like a bag for my dog.

Kate   But Edith, the dog is in England!

(Im Restaurant...)

Kellner Der Fisch ist nicht auf der Speisekarte und der Nachtisch ist heute Apfelstrudel mit Eis oder Sahne.

Horst Frau Walker, kann ich Ihnen helfen? Vielleicht eine Suppe... und dann danach?

Kate Ich möchte gern das Steak mit Salat, bitte.

Edith Ich glaube, zuviel rotes Fleisch ist nicht gut für Sie, Kate.

Horst Herr Walker, was können wir Ihnen geben? Und was möchten Sie trinken? Wein?

Tom Ich möchte lieber ein Bier und dann die Bratwurst, mit Kartoffeln und Gemüse, bitte.

Edith Tom, das Gemüse ist in Sahne. Ich möchte das nicht essen.

Horst Und Sie, Frau Palmer?

Edith Ein bisschen Huhn vom Grill, Obst und ein Glas Wasser, bitte.

(Später...)

Horst Sind wir alle fertig? Es ist spät. Möchte jemand eine Tasse Kaffee? Niemand? Gut, die Rechnung, bitte.

Edith Oh, Herr Schmidt, können Sie mir bitte helfen! Wie sagt man auf Deutsch 'doggy bag'? Ich möchte eine Tüte für meinen Hund.

Kate Aber Edith, der Hund ist in England!

New words

◀)) CD2, tr 5

jemand someone
er he
sagen/gesagt say/said
warum why
Nummer number
auf on
Papier paper
bei, beim at, at the
Buch book
Herr Mr, gentleman
Kunde client
kennen to know
ihn, ihm him
Donnerstag Thursday
Termin appointment
wichtig important
Sache matter, thing
danke thank you
sicher sure, certainly
möglich possible
nächste Woche next week
natürlich of course
interessant interesting
Zeit time
wunderbar wonderful
ein paar a few
ach so I see
oben at the top, upstairs
an at
Ausgang exit
Tür door

Dienstag Tuesday
vielen Dank thank you very much
hinter behind
Kirche church
gemütlich comfortable, cosy
unser, unsere our
sie weiss/wissen she knows/ know (something)
Hund dog
krank sick
schwer heavy, difficult
Erkältung cold
Schmerzen pains
Arzt doctor
kommen come
das geht nicht that's not possible, that's not on
Fisch fish
Speisekarte menu
Nachtisch dessert
Eis ice cream
Ihnen you
helfen/geholfen help/helped
Suppe soup
gern gladly, very much
Salat salad
Fleisch meat
geben/gegeben give/given
lieber rather (i.e. prefer)
Bratwurst fried sausage

Gemüse vegetables
Huhn chicken
Obst fruit
Glas glass
Wasser water

fertig ready
niemand nobody
**wie sagt man... auf
Deutsch?** how do you say...
in German?

> **TOTAL NEW WORDS: 67
> ... only 85 words to go!**

Some easy extras

The days of the week

Montag Monday
Dienstag Tuesday
Mittwoch Wednesday
Donnerstag Thursday

Freitag Friday
Sonnabend/Samstag
Saturday
Sonntag Sunday

Good news grammar

◀》 CD2, tr 6

1 The future: more good news

In colloquial German there is no difference between: *I am sick*
Ich bin krank and *I am going to be sick tomorrow* **Ich bin
morgen krank**.

So when you are talking about things that are *going to happen*,
there's no need to add frills like *shall*, *will* or *going to*. Just add
morgen or **Donnerstag** or any other word that indicates that the
action is going to happen in the future.

2 *Gern* and *lieber*: easy!

If you want to say that you *like* doing something or *enjoy* doing it you
use **gern**:

Ich helfe Jim gern. *I like helping Jim.* **Ich spreche gern Deutsch.**
I enjoy speaking German.

If you want to say that you *prefer* doing something you use **lieber**:

Ich helfe lieber Paula. *I prefer helping Paula.*
Ich spreche lieber Deutsch. *I prefer speaking German.*

3 Pronouns: very useful

These are the little words which save you repeating the name of the
person or thing you are talking about: *Tom said to Kate that he was
going to meet **her***, as opposed to *Tom said to Kate that Tom was
going to meet Kate.*

Here are the personal pronouns you'll learn in **Fast German with
Elisabeth Smith**:

I	*you*	*he*	*she*	*it*	*we*	*they*	*me*
ich	Sie/Ihnen	er	sie	es	wir	sie	mich/mir
	him		*her*	*us*		*them*	
	ihn/ihm		sie/ihr	uns		sie/ihnen	

This may look like a bit of a minefield, especially when there are two
choices for the same word. But amazingly, you will learn to pick the
right one most of the time.

4 The third person (just like in English)

When you are talking about another person or about something, you often have to change the verb, just like you do in English.

Example   I *eat* – Tom *eats*. Ich **esse** – Tom **isst**.

I *have* – it *has*. Ich *habe* – es **hat**.

In Week 2, you learned about dropping the **n** when saying **ich**, so this is just another small step.

When in doubt, remember you'll find all the verbs in Week 6.

Learn by heart

🔊 CD2, tr 7

Pretend this is a one-sided telephone call by a rather opinionated person. When you know it, act it out in less than 50 seconds.

Möchten Sie mit mir essen gehen?
Möchten Sie Freitag abend mit mir essen gehen?
Ich kenne ein sehr gemütliches Restaurant.
Man kann da viele gute Sachen essen, und der Wein ist wunderbar.
Nein, Sie möchten nicht? Warum nicht? Ich bin sehr interessant!
Sie kennen mich nicht?
Aber sicher, Sie sehen mich immer im Fernsehen: Ich mache das Wetter.
Sie können nicht? Warum nicht?
Sie haben einen wichtigen Termin?
Das ist nicht möglich!

Say it simply

When people want to speak German but don't dare it's usually because they are trying to translate what they want to say from English into German. But because they don't know some of the words they give up.

With **Fast German with Elisabeth Smith** you work around the words you don't know with the words you know. And 356 words is enough to say anything. It may not be very elegant – but who cares? You are *communicating*!

Here are two examples showing you how to say things simply.

1 You need to change your flight from Tuesday to Friday.

Say it simply:

Wir können nicht Dienstag fliegen, wir möchten Freitag fliegen.
We cannot fly Tuesday, we would like to fly Friday.

or:

Dienstag ist nicht gut für uns. Wir möchten den Flug am Freitag.
Tuesday is not good for us. We would like the flight on Friday.

2 This time your friend has just broken the heel of her only pair of shoes. You have to catch a train and need some help now.

Say it simply:

Entschuldigen Sie, der Schuh hier ist kaputt. Gibt es hier ein Geschäft, wo man das sehr schnell repariert?
Excuse me, the shoe here is broken. Is there a shop here, where one can repair that very quickly?

Let's speak German

🔊 CD2, tr 8

Here are ten sentences as a warm-up and then on to greater things.

1 Who has said that?
2 I don't know why.
3 Can I help you?
4 I believe we have time later.
5 I enjoy driving to Hamburg.
6 He would like to know that.
7 Work on Sunday? That's not on!
8 Can I give you my number?
9 I prefer to eat chicken.
10 Yes, sure, I have an appointment for you.

Now pretend you are in Germany with friends who do not speak German. They will want you to ask people things in German. They will say: *Please ask him...*

11 if he knows Edith Palmer
12 if he is going to eat with us on Tuesday
13 if she would like meat or fish and potatoes
14 if they have an appointment today
15 if they know where the restaurant is

Now your friends ask you to tell people things. This time they use some words you don't know, so you have to work round it by using the ones you do. They say: *Please tell him...*

16 that the soup is stone cold
17 that we are unfortunately in a rush now
18 that we would like to have a meal with them
19 that I am a vegetarian
20 that next week will suit us

Answers

1 Wer hat das gesagt?
2 Ich weiss nicht warum.
3 Kann ich Ihnen helfen?
4 Ich glaube, wir haben später Zeit.
5 Ich fahre gern nach Hamburg.
6 Er möchte das gern wissen.
7 Sonntag arbeiten? Das geht nicht!
8 Kann ich Ihnen meine Nummer geben?
9 Ich esse lieber Huhn.
10 Ja sicher, ich habe einen Termin für Sie.
11 Kennen Sie Edith Palmer?
12 Essen Sie Dienstag mit uns?
13 Möchten Sie Fleisch oder Fisch und Kartoffeln?
14 Haben Sie heute einen Termin?
15 Wissen Sie, wo das Restaurant ist?
16 Die Suppe ist sehr kalt.
17 Wir haben jetzt leider keine Zeit.
18 Wir möchten (gern) mit Ihnen essen.
19 Er/sie isst kein Fleisch.
20 Nächste Woche ist gut für uns.

Let's speak more German

◀》 CD2, tr 9

In your own words

This exercise will teach you to express yourself freely. Use only the words you have learned so far.

Tell me in your own words that...

1 you spoke on the phone with Horst Schmidt
2 you saw the number in the phonebook
3 you want to know if I know him
4 he is a good and important client
5 an appointment with him next week is a possibility
6 you are going for dinner with Horst on Saturday
7 Edith Palmer cannot come; she has a cold
8 you are keen to eat sausage and potato salad
9 nobody would like to drink water
10 the evening was wonderful and very interesting

Answers

1 Ich habe mit Horst Schmidt telefoniert.
2 Ich habe die Nummer im Telefonbuch gesehen.
3 Kennen Sie ihn?
4 Er is ein guter und wichtiger Kunde.
5 Ein Termin mit ihm nächste Woche ist möglich.
6 Ich gehe mit Horst am Sonnabend essen.
7 Edith Palmer kann nicht kommen. Sie hat eine Erkältung.
8 Ich möchte Wurst und Kartoffelsalat essen.
9 Niemand möchte Wasser trinken.
10 Der Abend war wunderbar und sehr interessant.

Let's speak German – fast and fluently

◀》 CD2, tr 10

Translate each section and check if it is correct, then cover up the answers and say the three or four sentences fast.

Try to say each group of sentences in less than 20 seconds.

Do you know Horst Schmidt? He phoned today.
Why? He said it wasn't important.
It was for an appointment on Wednesday.

Kennen Sie Horst Schmidt? Er hat heute telefoniert.
Warum? Er hat gesagt, es war nicht wichtig.
Es war für einen Termin am Mittwoch.

Horst is only a few days in Berlin.
There is a restaurant; It is new, by the bank.
I would like with him there to eat.

Horst ist nur ein paar Tage in Berlin.
Es gibt ein Restaurant; es ist neu, bei der Bank.
Ich möchte mit ihm da essen.

Would you like also to come?
No, I believe that's unfortunately not possible.
My dog is ill. He has pains. I have him too much meat given.
I see. Of course. I'm sorry.

Möchten Sie auch kommen?
Nein, ich glaube, das ist leider nicht möglich/das geht leider nicht.
Mein Hund ist krank. Er hat Schmerzen. Ich habe ihm zuviel
Fleisch gegeben.
Ach so. Natürlich. Es tut mir Leid.

Spot the keys

◀))) CD2, tr 11

Now you are in a department store and ask the sales assistant if the black shoes you fancy were also available in size 39:

YOU   **Entschuldigen Sie, haben Sie diese Schuhe auch in Grösse 39?**

She said **nein** then **einen Moment bitte** and went into the stockroom. When she came back this is what she said:

ANSWER   *Alsoichhabeebennoch inunserem Lager angerufendassdienochmalnachkucken aberdiehabendie* **Schuhe** *nur nochin* **braun.** *Aberichweissaus Erfahrungdassdiese Markeoft* **sehr gross** *ausfälltundichmeine* **Grösse achtunddreissig** *wäreeventuell* **gross genug.**

Size 39 was only available in brown but size 38 should be big enough.

Test your progress

1 I am sure our appointment was (on) Tuesday.
2 Today? No, that is not possible. Unfortunately, we do not have time.
3 I must buy a few things for my friends.
4 Can you help me please? I would like the number of the doctor.
5 Do you know where there is a good restaurant?
6 I believe the church is very interesting, but nobody would like to see it.
7 We would like to fly next Monday evening.
8 Can you give me the menu, please?
9 Have you given him your papers?
10 Can one buy fruit and vegetables here?
11 Do you know his new book?
12 It was wonderful, thank you very much for the nice evening!
13 Why must you see my credit card?
14 The two weeks on the QE II were a little boring.
15 You see the cashpoint machine upstairs at the exit, by the door.
16 We eat chicken or fried sausage – the fish is too expensive.
17 How does one say in German…?
18 Do you know where there is a bus here?
19 My husband likes going to Texas, but I prefer going to Arizona.
20 They did not say where this cosy restaurant was.

There were eight split verbs in this test. Did you spot them? Check your answers. Another brilliant score on the chart?

Well on the way

After four weeks you are well on the way, and as a reward for all your hard work here's a bit of light relief – a multiple-choice quiz. Try to score 8 out of 10.

1 What would you expect to be offered in Germany for breakfast?

    a Salami   **c** Käse

    b Schinken   **d** Orangenmarmelade

2 How do you say *half past 12* in German?

    a halb zwölf   **c** halb elf

    b halb eins   **d** halb nach zwölf

3 How would Herr Schmidt and Frau Schulze address each other after having been good neighbours for ten years?

    a Helmut and Karin   **c** Herr Schmidt and Frau Schulze

    b Liebling

4 How do you say and spell *sales assistant* in German?

    a verkaufer   **c** Verkäufer

    b Verkeufer   **d** Kellner

5 When do you exchange Christmas presents in Germany?

    a Heiligabend (24th)   **c** am ersten Weihnachtstag,

    b am ersten Weihnachtstag   abends

        (25th), morgens

6 What's wrong? **Ich habe gekauft den Wein am Sonntag bei Karstadt.**

    a gekauft muss ans Ende   **c** alles

    b nichts

7 What does **es gibt** mean?

    a It gives   **c** there is, there are

    b does he give?

8 What is *New Year's Eve* in German and what happens at midnight?

    a Ostern/nichts   **c** Pfingsten/arbeiten

    b Sylvester/grosses Feuerwerk

9 How do you say in German *I am sorry*?

    a Es tut mir Leid   **c** kein Problem

    b ach, du meine Güte

10 What do Germans do when they meet?

    a lachen   **c** geben sich die Hand

    b küssen   **d** nichts

Answers

1 a, b, c   2 b   3 c   4 c   5 a   6 a, c (stores are not open on Sunday)

7 a, c   8 b   9 a   10 c

Week 5

Day-by-day guide

How about 15 minutes on the train, tube or bus, 10 minutes on the way home and 20 minutes before switching on the television…?

Day one
- Read **On the move**.
- Listen to/Read **Unterwegs**.
- Learn 15+.

Day two
- Repeat **Unterwegs**.
- Read the **New words**.
- Cut out the **Flash words** and get stuck in.

Day three
- Test yourself to perfection on all the **New words**.
- Read and learn **Good news grammar**.

Day four
- Cut out and learn the ten **Flash sentences**.
- Listen to/Read **Learn by heart**.

Day five
- Listen to/Read **Let's speak German**.
- Listen to/Read **Spot the keys**.

Day six
- Listen to/Read **Let's speak more German** (optional).
- Listen to/Read **Let's speak German – fast and fluently** (optional).
- Translate **Test your progress**.

Day seven
I bet you don't want a day off… but I insist!

On the move

Tom and Kate travel through Bavaria by train, bus and hire car.

(At the station...)

Tom   Two tickets please to Lake Starnberg.

Clerk   Thereandback?

Tom   There and what? Can you speak slowly, please?

Clerk   There – and – back?

Tom   Only there, please. When does the train go and where (from)?

Clerk   Nine forty-five, platform eight.

Kate   Quick, Tom, here are two seats in the non-smoking.* Oh, someone is smoking there. Excuse me, you cannot smoke here, because this is 'non-smoking'. Smoking is forbidden here.

Man   Sorry, I don't understand. I only speak English.

(At the bus stop...)

Kate   On a Sunday the bus does not come often. We have to wait for 20 minutes. Tom, here are my postcards and a letter. There is a letterbox down there. I am taking a few photos. The lake is so beautiful in the sun.

Tom   Kate, quickly, two buses are coming. Both are blue. This one is full. We take the other one. *(In the bus...)* Two to Munich, please.

Driver   This bus goes to Lake Starnberg only.

Tom   But we are at Lake Starnberg.

Driver   Yes, yes, but this is the bus for the Starnberg hospital.

(In the car...)

Tom   Here comes our car. Only 100 euros for three days. I am very pleased.

Kate   I do not like the car. I think it was so cheap because it is very old. I hope that we are not going to have problems.

---

* Please note that smoking is no longer permitted in any compartment on

Unterwegs

🔊 CD2, tr 4

Tom and Kate travel through Bavaria by train, bus and hire car.

(Am Bahnhof...)

Tom   Zwei Fahrkarten bitte zum Starnberger See.

Clerk   Hinundzurück?

Tom   Hin und was? Können Sie bitte langsam sprechen?

Clerk   Hin – und – zurück?

Tom   Nur hin, bitte. Wann fährt der Zug und wo?

Clerk   Neun Uhr fünfundvierzig, Gleis acht.

Kate   Schnell, Tom, hier sind zwei Plätze im Nichtraucher.
Oh, da raucht jemand. Entschuldigen Sie, Sie können hier
nicht rauchen, denn dies ist kein Raucher. Rauchen ist hier
verboten.

Man   Sorry, I don't understand. Ich spreche only English.

(An der Bushaltestelle...)

Kate   Am Sonntag kommt der Bus nicht oft. Wir müssen zwanzig
Minuten warten. Tom, hier sind meine Karten und ein Brief.
Da unten ist ein Briefkasten. Ich mache ein paar Fotos.
Der See ist so schön in der Sonne.

Tom   Kate, schnell, zwei Busse kommen. Beide sind blau. Dieser
ist voll. Wir nehmen den anderen. *(Im Bus...)* Zweimal nach
München bitte.

Driver Dieser Bus fährt nur zum Starnberger See.

Tom   Aber wir sind am Starnberger See.

Driver Ja, ja, aber dies ist der Bus zum Starnberger Krankenhaus.

(Im Auto...)

Tom   Hier kommt unser Auto. Nur hundert Euro für drei Tage.
Ich bin sehr zufrieden.

Kate   Das Auto gefällt mir nicht. Ich glaube es war so billig, weil es
sehr alt ist. Ich hoffe, dass wir keine Probleme haben.

Tom   The first car was too expensive, the second one too big. This was the last. (*Later...*) Where are we? The map has gone. On the left is a petrol station and a stop for the underground and on the right is a school. Quickly!

Kate   The main road is at the traffic light. If we go to the end we'll come to the motorway. Perhaps three kilometres. (*On the motorway...*) Why does the car go so slowly? Do we have enough petrol? How many litres? Do we have oil? Is the engine hot? I think the car 'has had it'. Where is the mobile phone? Where is the number of the workshop? Where is my bag?

Tom   Kate, these questions are making me mad. And here comes the rain! And why are the police behind us?

Tom   Das erste Auto war zu teuer und das zweite zu gross. Dies war das letzte. (*Später…*) Wo sind wir? Die Karte ist weg. Links sind eine Tankstelle und eine U-Bahn Haltestelle und rechts ist eine Schule. Schnell!

Kate   Die Hauptstrasse ist bei der Ampel. Wenn wir bis zum Ende fahren, kommen wir zur Autobahn. Vielleicht drei Kilometer. (*Auf der Autobahn...*) Warum fährt das Auto so langsam? Haben wir genug Benzin? Wieviel Liter? Haben wir Öl? Ist der Motor heiss? Ich glaube das Auto ist kaputt. Wo ist das Handy? Wo ist die Nummer von der Werkstatt? Wo ist meine Tasche?

Tom   Kate, diese Fragen machen mich verrückt. Und hier kommt der Regen. Und warum ist die Polizei hinter uns?

New words

🔊 CD2, tr 13

unterwegs on the move
Bahnhof (railway) station
Fahrkarte ticket
hin und zurück there and
  back, return (ticket)
langsam slow, slowly
sprechen/gesprochen speak
  spoken
Zug train
Gleis track, platform
schnell quick, quickly
Nichtraucher non-smoker,
  non-smoking (compartment)
rauchen smoke
denn because
Raucher smoker, smoking
  (compartment)
verboten forbidden
Haltestelle stop
oft often
warten/gewartet wait/waited
Karte card, postcard, map
Brief letter
(da) unten down (there), at the
  bottom
Kasten box
Foto photo
See lake, sea
Sonne sun
beide both
voll full
nehmen/genommen take/taken
anderer, andere other, other one
zweimal twice

Krankenhaus hospital
Auto car
Tag, Tage day, days
zufrieden content, happy
es gefällt mir nicht I don't like it
  (it pleases me not)
weil because
alt old
hoffen hope
dass that
erste first
zweite second
letzte last
weg gone
Tankstelle petrol station
U-Bahn underground
Schule school
Hauptstrasse main road
Ampel traffic light
wenn if, when
Ende end
Autobahn motorway
Kilometer kilometre
Benzin petrol
Liter litre
Öl oil
Motor engine
heiss hot
Werkstatt workshop,
  garage
Tasche bag
Regen rain
Polizei police, police station
uns us

TOTAL NEW WORDS: 61
... only 24 words to go!

Easy extras

Es gefällt mir. I like it (literally: *it pleases me*).

Es gefällt mir nicht. I do not like it (literally: *it pleases me not*).

Das Auto gefällt mir. I like the car. (*The car pleases me.*)

Das Auto gefällt uns nicht. We do not like the car. (*The car does not please us.*)

Good news grammar

🔊 CD2, tr 14

1 *Dass* (that), *weil* (because), *wenn* (if, when)

- Ich hoffe, **dass** wir keine Probleme **haben**.
  I hope that we don't have problems.
- Das Auto ist so billig, **weil** es so alt **ist**.
  The car is so cheap because it is so old.
- Wir haben kein Geld mehr, **wenn** wir das Haus gekauft **haben**.
  We don't (won't) have any more money when we (we'll) have bought the house.

Can you see that after **dass, weil** or **wenn** the verb goes to the end? And **haben gekauft** does an extra twist, becoming **gekauft haben**. Don't shoot the messenger!

If you get the words in the wrong order – it's not a problem because people will still understand you.

Good news: another word for *because* is **denn**. There is no change in word order after **denn: Das Auto ist billig, denn es ist alt.** *The car is cheap because it is old.* Good old **denn**! Use it!

2 Another twist

Here's a harmless-looking sentence: *First we eat fish.* This should be: **Zuerst wir essen Fisch.** But instead it is: **Zuerst essen wir Fisch.**

This sentence doesn't start with the subject (*we*), so the verb (**essen**) has rushed into second place. *First eat we fish.* Remember: **Da raucht jemand.** *Someone is smoking there.* **Am Sonntag kommt der Bus.** *The bus is coming on Sunday?* But if you say **Am Sonntag der Bus kommt**, it's near enough!

Learn by heart

🔊 CD2, tr 15

Here's a dialogue between someone who pranged the car and someone else who is getting suspicious! Try to say the ten lines like a prize-winning one-act play. I challenge you to 45 seconds.

Das Auto ist nur ein bisschen kaputt!
Können wir morgen zum Tennis gehen?
Jemand hat mir Karten gegeben.
Ich möchte die zwei neuen Amerikaner sehen.
Und können wir die U-Bahn nehmen?
Oder besser den Bus, weil er genau zum Tennisplatz fährt.

Bus? U-Bahn? Warum? Die Sache gefällt mir nicht.
Wir haben unten ein schönes Auto.

Ja, also… ich habe nicht gesehen, dass die Ampel rot war…
Aber das Auto ist nur ein bisschen kaputt!

Let's speak German

🔊 CD2, tr 16

Here's your ten-point warm-up: I give you an answer and you ask me a question, as if you did not hear the words in bold very well.

Example Steffie ist **hier**. *Question* **Wo ist Steffie?**

1 Das Handy ist **in meiner Tasche**.
2 Die **Autobahn** ist da unten.
3 Der Bus kommt **in zwanzig Minuten**.
4 **Tom** möchte mit Herrn Schmidt sprechen.
5 Hin und zurück nach Köln kostet **30 Euro**.
6 Das Haus gefällt mir nicht, **weil** es sehr alt ist.
7 Sie kommen **mit dem Auto** nach England.
8 Ich habe **die Ampel** nicht gesehen.
9 **Ja**, das Hotel gefällt mir.
10 **Nein**, ich bin mit der Schule nicht zufrieden.

Now answer, starting with **ja** and **ich**:

11 Kennen Sie die neue Autobahn?
12 Nehmen Sie diesen Bus?
13 Gehen Sie jetzt zum Bahnhof?
14 Gefällt Ihnen der See?
15 Können Sie die Haltestelle sehen?

Here are five things you want to refer to but you don't know what they are called in German. Explain them using the words you know.

16 your parents-in-law
17 central heating
18 a headache
19 a teacher
20 kennels

Answers

1 Wo ist das Handy?
2 Was ist da unten?
3 Wann kommt der Bus?
4 Wer möchte mit Herrn Schmidt sprechen?
5 Wieviel kostet es nach Köln?
6 Warum gefällt Ihnen das Haus nicht?
7 Wie kommen sie nach England?
8 Was haben Sie nicht gesehen?
9 Gefällt Ihnen das Hotel?
10 Sind Sie mit der Schule zufrieden?
11 Ja, ich kenne die neue Autobahn.
12 Ja, Ich nehme diesen Bus.
13 Ja, ich gehe jetzt zum Bahnhof.
14 Ja, der See gefällt mir.
15 Ja, ich kann die Haltestelle sehen.
16 Die Eltern von meinem Mann/von meiner Frau.
17 Es macht alle Zimmer im Haus warm.
18 Schmerzen hier oben.
19 Der Mann oder die Frau in der Schule. Sie arbeiten mit den Kindern.
20 Ein Haus für Hunde, wenn wir Urlaub haben.

Let's speak more German

🔊 CD2, tr 17

In your own words

This exercise will teach you to express yourself freely. Use only the words you have learned so far.

Tell me in your own words that...

1 you bought a return ticket to Lake Constance (Bodensee)
2 you believe the train goes from platform seven at 10.15
3 you have a seat in non-smoking
4 on Monday you wouldn't mind going by bus to Stuttgart
5 you must take some photos for your company
6 the first bus is 'chock-a-block'; you take the other one
7 your car is coming on Thursday; it is new but very cheap
8 your wife says: 'It's terrible, I don't like it.'
9 she says the car is too slow and the engine always overheats
10 hopefully you won't have problems

Answers

1 Ich habe eine Fahrkarte zum Bodensee gekauft. Hin und zurück.

2 Ich glaube der Zug fährt/geht von Gleis sieben um viertel nach zehn/zehn Uhr fünfzehn.

3 Ich habe einen Platz im Nichtraucher.

4 Am Montag möchte ich mit dem Bus nach Stuttgart fahren.

5 Ich muss Fotos für meine Firma machen.

6 Der erste Bus ist voll. Ich nehme den anderen.

7 Mein Auto kommt am Donnerstag. Es ist neu aber sehr billig.

8 Meine Frau sagt: 'Es ist schrecklich, es gefällt mir nicht.'

9 Sie sagt das Auto ist zu langsam und der Motor ist immer heiss.

10 Ich hoffe, dass ich keine Probleme habe. Or: Wir hoffen, dass wir keine Probleme haben.

Let's speak German – fast and fluently

🔊 CD2, tr 18

Translate each section and check if it is correct, then cover up the answers and say the three or four sentences fast! Try to say each group of sentences in less than 25 seconds.

Some of the English is in 'German-speak' to help you.

A ticket to Frankfurt, please. Only one way.
How much? Excuse me, can you speak slowly, please?
Yes, I would like a ticket for today.

Eine Fahrkarte nach Frankfurt, bitte. Nur hin.
Wieviel? Entschuldigen Sie, können Sie bitte langsam sprechen?
Ja, ich möchte eine Fahrkarte für heute.

My wife is taking a photo of the letterbox.
It is yellow not red like in England.
But it is full.
What are we going to do with the postcards?

Meine Frau macht ein Foto vom Briefkasten.
Er ist gelb, nicht rot wie in England.
Aber er ist voll.
Was machen wir mit den Postkarten?

We don't have a map of the centre.
I can't see the main road to the motorway.
All the traffic lights are not working.
My wife has a cold.
And who has taken my mobile phone?

Wir haben keine Karte vom Zentrum.
Ich kann die Hauptstrasse zur Autobahn nicht sehen.
Alle Ampeln sind kaputt.
Meine Frau hat eine Erkältung.
Und wer hat mein Handy genommen?

Spot the keys

🔊 CD2, tr 19

This time you are planning a trip in the country and want to have some idea what the weather will be like. This is what you would ask:

YOU **Entschuldigen Sie, können Sie mir bitte sagen, was für Wetter wir morgen haben?**

ANSWER *Ja,* **ich weiss nicht,** *ob die letzte* **Wetter** *vorhersage* **im Fernsehen** *stimmt,* **aber** *danachsolldas Tiefdruckgebiet* **langsam** *abziehen, unddessoll* **morgen warm** *werden, alsoüber* **fünfundzwanzig** *Grad* **aber** *eventuellkriegenwirdoch wieder* **Regen am Abend.**

He isn't sure but according to the TV something slow is happening (?) and it will be warm tomorrow – 25°C – but with rain again in the evening.

Test your progress

Translate into German.

1 I don't like this bag, the other bag was better.

2 How much does the ticket cost – return?

3 What did you say? Can you speak slowly, please?

4 I know that petrol is cheaper in America.

5 It is forbidden to smoke in the underground.

6 I cannot wait, I have a second appointment at eleven o'clock.

7 Is this box for letters? A yellow letterbox?

8 Hello, we are 30 km from Hanover, is that the garage?

9 Which is faster: the train or the car on the motorway?

10 It is very hot this week. I would rather (have) a little rain.

11 He did not see the traffic light and now they are both in hospital.

12 I saw her twice at the petrol station today. Her car drinks petrol!

13 Where is there a dry cleaner's? I have oil on my Armani T-shirt.

14 We live behind the main road, exactly at the bus stop.

15 We are at the police station because our mobile phone has gone.

16 The tickets are cheaper if you buy them now.

17 I like your car. Was it very expensive?

18 Can you help us please? Where can one eat here by the lake?

If you know all your words you should score over 90%.

Week 6

Day-by-day guide

This is your last week. Need I say more?

Day one
- Read **In the airport**.
- Listen to/Read **Im Flughafen**.
- Read the **New words** (only 24!).

Day two
- Repeat **Im Flughafen** and learn all the **New words**.
- Start working with the **Flash sentences**.

Day three
- Test yourself on the **Flash sentences**.
- Listen to/Read **Learn by heart**.

Day four
- No more grammar. Have a look at the summary.
- Read **Say it simply**.

Day five
- Listen to/Read **Spot the keys**.
- Listen to/Read **Let's speak German**.

Day six
- Listen to/Read **Let's speak more German** (optional).
- Listen to/Read **Let's speak German – fast and fluently** (optional).
- Your last **Test your progress**. Go for it!

Day seven

> **Congratulations!**
> **You have successfully completed the course**
> **and can now speak**
> *Fast German with Elisabeth Smith!*

In the airport

It's the end of the trip and time to go home. There's one more surprise for Tom and Kate when they bump into an old friend in the departure lounge.

Tom On Monday we have to work. Terrible. I would like to go to Italy now or fly from here to Hawaii. My company can wait and nobody knows where I am.

Kate And what are the people in my office going to say? They wait for two days and then they'll phone and speak to my mother. I am sure she'll give them the number of my mobile phone. And then?

Tom Yes, yes, I know. Well, perhaps at Christmas, a week in the snow or on a boat to Madeira. I'll go and buy a newspaper downstairs... Kate! Here is Klaus Becker.

Klaus Hello. How are you? What are you doing here? This is my wife Nancy. Are your holidays finished? How was it?

Kate Germany was wonderful. We have seen a lot and eaten too much. We now know Bavaria and the Black Forest well.

Klaus Next year you must go to the Rhine. Mrs Walker, my wife would like to buy a book for our computer. Could you perhaps go with her and help her? And Mr Walker, you have a newspaper. Could you give me the Sport please? And then would you like to have a Schnaps?

(At the airport kiosk...)

Kate I see nothing here. What I see is not right. Are you also flying to England?

Nancy No, we are flying to Hamburg. Klaus's mother lives there. She had our children for two weeks. A boy and three girls. We are coming back by train tomorrow. That is cheaper.

Kate Your husband works at the Deutsche Bank?

Im Flughafen

🔊 CD2, tr 20

It's the end of the trip and time to go home. There's one more surprise for Tom and Kate when they bump into an old friend in the departure lounge.

Tom   Montag müssen wir arbeiten. Schrecklich. Ich möchte jetzt nach Italien fahren oder von hier nach Hawaii fliegen. Meine Firma kann warten und niemand weiss, wo ich bin.

Kate   Und was sagen die Leute in meiner Firma? Sie warten zwei Tage und dann telefonieren sie und sprechen mit meiner Mutter. Sie gibt Ihnen sicher die Nummer von meinem Handy. Und dann?

Tom   Ja, ja, ich weiss. Also vielleicht Weihnachten eine Woche im Schnee oder mit einem Schiff nach Madeira. Ich gehe unten eine Zeitung kaufen… Kate! Hier ist Klaus Becker.

Klaus   Hallo. Wie geht's? Was machen Sie hier? Dies ist meine Frau, Nancy. Ist Ihr Urlaub zuende? Wie war es?

Kate   Deutschland war wunderbar. Wir haben viel gesehen und zuviel gegessen. Wir kennen Bayern und den Schwarzwald jetzt gut.

Klaus   Nächstes Jahr müssen Sie an den Rhein fahren. Frau Walker, meine Frau möchte ein Buch für unseren Computer kaufen. Können Sie vielleicht mit ihr gehen und ihr helfen? Und Herr Walker, Sie haben eine Zeitung. Können Sie mir bitte den Sport geben? Und möchten Sie dann einen Schnaps trinken?

(Am Kiosk vom Flughafen…)

Kate   Ich sehe hier nichts. Was ich sehe, ist nicht richtig. Fliegen Sie auch nach England?

Nancy   Nein, wir fliegen nach Hamburg. Die Mutter von Klaus wohnt da. Sie hatte unsere Kinder für zwei Wochen. Ein Junge und drei Mädchen. Wir kommen morgen mit dem Zug zurück. Das ist billiger.

Kate   Ihr Mann arbeitet bei der Deutschen Bank?

Nancy   Yes, his job is interesting but the money is not good.
            Our VW is nine years old and we have a small old flat. We
            had a lot to repair this year. My parents and my girlfriend are
            in the USA and we write a lot of letters. I would very much
            like to fly to America but that costs too much money.

Kate   But you have a beautiful house in Mallorca.

Nancy   A house in Mallorca? I have never been to Mallorca. When we
            have a holiday, we go to the Ruhrgebiet to a friend.

Tom   Kate, come, we must (go) to our flight. Goodbye… What is the
            matter, Kate? What did Mrs Becker say?

Kate   Wait, Tom, wait...

Nancy Ja, sein Job ist interessant, aber das Geld ist nicht gut. Unser VW ist neun Jahre alt, und wir haben eine kleine alte Wohnung. Wir hatten dieses Jahr viel zu reparieren. Meine Eltern und meine Freundin sind in den USA und wir schreiben viele Briefe. Ich möchte gern nach Amerika fliegen, aber das kostet zu viel Geld.

Kate Aber Sie haben ein schönes Haus auf Mallorca.

Nancy Ein Haus auf Mallorca? Ich war nie auf Mallorca. Wenn wir Urlaub haben, fahren wir ins Ruhrgebiet zu einem Freund.

Tom Kate, komm, wir müssen zu unserem Flug. Auf Wiedersehen… Was ist los, Kate? Was hat Frau Becker gesagt?

Kate Warte, Tom, warte,,,

New words

🔊 CD2, tr 21

Flughafen airport
Leute people
Mutter mother
ihnen them
Weihnachten Christmas
Schnee snow
Schiff ship
wie geht's? how are you?
zuende finished, over
Deutschland Germany
ihr her
nichts nothing
richtig right

wohnen live
sie hatte/hatten she had/
  they had
Junge boy
Mädchen girl
sein his
Wohnung apartment, flat
schreiben write
nie never
Ruhrgebiet industrial area of
  Germany
Flug flight
was ist los? what is the matter?

> **TOTAL NEW WORDS: 24**
> **Total German words learned: 356**
> **Extra words: 67**
> **GRAND TOTAL: 423**

Learn by heart

🔊 CD2, tr 22

This is your last dialogue to learn by heart. Give it your best.

You now have a large store of everyday German which will be very useful.

Auf Wiedersehen

Kate Herr Schmidt, Kate Walker hier, vom Flughafen Frankfurt. Ja, unser Urlaub ist leider zuende und unser Geld auch. Vielen Dank für den schönen Abend! Tom möohte mit Ihnen sprechen, auf Wiedersehen!

Tom Hallo Horst!... Was? Sie kaufen beide? Meine Firma hat Ihre E-mail? Das ist wunderbar. Vielen Dank! Nächstes Jahr?... Kate möchte nach Italien, aber ich komme lieber nach Deutschland. Mit Edith Palmer? Ach, du meine Güte, nein, nein! Unser Flugzeug wartet. Also... auf Wiedersehen!

Good news grammar

Here is a summary of all 32 verbs and verb forms. If you are brave
why not test yourself? Cover up the three columns on the right and
see how many you can remember.

Basic form			Past
Sie/wir/sie (they)	ich	er/sie (she)/es	
arbeiten	arbeite	arbeitet	gearbeitet
einkaufen/kaufen ein	kaufe ein	kauft ein	eingekauft
essen	esse	isst	gegessen
fahren	fahre	fährt	
fliegen	fliege	fliegt	
geben	gebe	gibt	gegeben
gehen	gehe	geht	
glauben	glaube	glaubt	geglaubt
haben	habe	hat	gehabt, *or* hatten, hatte
helfen	helfe	hilft	geholfen
hoffen	hoffe	hofft	gehofft
kaufen	kaufe	kauft	gekauft
kennen	kenne	kennt	gekannt
kommen	komme	kommt	
können	kann	kann	gekonnt
kosten	koste	kostet	gekostet
machen	mache	macht	gemacht
möchten	möchte	möchte	gemocht
müssen	muss	muss	gemusst
nehmen	nehme	nimmt	genommen
rauchen	rauche	raucht	geraucht
reparieren	repariere	repariert	repariert
sagen	sage	sagt	gesagt
schreiben	schreibe	schreibt	geschrieben
sehen	sehe	sieht	gesehen
sein/sind	bin	ist	*use:* war, waren
sprechen	spreche	spricht	gesprochen
telefonieren	telefoniere	telefoniert	telefoniert
trinken	trinke	trinkt	getrunken
warten	warte	wartet	gewartet
wissen	weiss	weiss	gewusst
wohnen	wohne	wohnt	gewohnt

Where you see a gap, the verb is rather irregular. So work around it
or use **war** or **waren** which are good stand-bys.

Say it simply

Here are two more exercises to practise using simple language:

1 You have just hired a car and notice a scratch on the left, behind the door. You want to report it so as not to get the bill for it later.

2 You are at the airport, about to catch your flight home when you realize that you have left some clothes behind in the room of your hotel. You phone the hotel's housekeeper to ask her to send the things on to you.

What would you say? Say it then write it down. Then compare your version against ours in the **Answers** section.

Spot the keys

◀)) CD2, tr 23

Here are two final practice rounds. If you have the recording, close the book now. Find the **Key words** and try to get the gist of it. Then take a look at the answers in the **Answers** section.

1 This is what you might ask a taxi driver:

YOU   **Wieviel Minuten ist es zum Flughafen und wieviel kostet es?**

ANSWER   *Es kommt darauf an, wann Sie fahren. Normalerweise dauert es zwanzig Minuten, aber wenn wir in den Verkehr kommen und die Bleichenbrücke ist dann völl verstopft, müssen Sie mit einer dreiviertel Stunde rechnen. Den Preis können Sie am Zähler ablesen. Normalerweise liegt er so zwischen 10 und 15 Euro.*

2 While in the departure lounge of the airport you hear someone raving about something. Identify the key words and work out where they have been.

'... und mein Mann hat auch gleich gesagt, es gefällt ihm weit aus besser hier. Und die Leute waren gar nicht so reserviert, wie man immer sagt, sondern sehr nett und weitaus höflicher als bei uns. Das Hotel lag direkt am See, und bei dem wunderbaren Wetter sind wir viel gewandert oder mit dem Auto durch die schöne Landschaft gefahren. Es gab da so viel interessantes zu sehen. Auch das Essen, wirklich gut. Also nächstes Jahr gehen wir garantiert zurück nach...'

Let's speak German

🔊 CD2, tr 24

Here's a five-point warm-up. Answer these questions using the words in brackets.

1 Hat er die Wohnung in Marbella gekauft? (Ja, Montag)
2 Wieviel Jahre haben Sie bei BMW gearbeitet? (drei)
3 Wann haben Sie mit Ihrer Firma gesprochen? (gestern)
4 Warum müssen Sie Ihr Auto immer reparieren? (weil, alt)
5 Hat er zuerst bei seiner Mutter gewohnt? (nein, bei seiner Freundin)

In your last exercise you are going to act as an interpreter again, this time telling your German friend what others have said in English.

Each time say the whole sentence out loud, translating the English words in brackets. Remember, after **wenn, dass** and **weil** all verbs go to the end of the sentence.

6 Jemand sagt, Sie sind verrückt,… (if you buy this old flat)
7 Jemand sagt, es gefällt ihm nicht,… (if you come too late)
8 Jemand sagt, es ist kaputt,… (if you have no hot water)
9 Meine Freundin hat gesagt,… (that our holiday is over)
10 Sie hat auch gesagt,… (that we will come back next year)
11 Meine Frau möchte sagen,… (that she has a cold)
12 Mein Mann sagt, er kann nicht kommen,… (because he works on a ship)
13 Er kann auch nicht kommen,… (because he is often sick)
14 Mein Freund sagt,… (that you are very beautiful)
15 Er sagt auch,… (that he would like your telephone number)

Let's speak German

87

Answers

1 **Ja, er hat Montag die Wohnung in Marbella gekauft.**
2 **Ich habe drei Jahre bei BMW gearbeitet.**
3 **Ich habe gestern mit meiner Firma gesprochen.**
4 **Ich muss mein Auto immer reparieren, weil es sehr alt ist.**
5 **Nein, er hat zuerst bei seiner Freundin gewohnt.**
6 **wenn Sie diese alte Wohnung kaufen.**
7 **wenn Sie zu spät kommen.**
8 **wenn sie kein heisses Wasser haben.**
9 **dass unser Urlaub zuende ist.**
10 **dass wir nächstes Jahr zurück kommen.**
11 **dass sie eine Erkältung hat.**
12 **weil er auf einem Schiff arbeitet.**
13 **weil er oft krank ist.**
14 **dass Sie sehr schön sind.**
15 **dass er Ihre Telefonnummer möchte.**

Now do it once more – as quickly as you can.

Let's speak more German

In your own words

This exercise will teach you to express yourself freely. Use only the words you have learned so far.

Tell me in your own words that…

1 next week you have to work
2 you don't like it; you'd rather have more leave
3 nobody knows that you are in Italy
4 your mother has the number of your mobile phone
5 your vacation was wonderful
6 you did a lot of sightseeing and eating
7 your friend Mr Becker is on his way to Hamburg today
8 he is returning by train tomorrow
9 your wife must fly to America, because her parents are ill
10 you would like to go to America for Christmas, but by boat

Answers

1 **Nächste Woche muss ich arbeiten.**
2 **Es gefällt mir nicht. Ich möchte lieber mehr Urlaub/Ferien haben.**
3 **Niemand weiss, dass ich in Italien bin.**
4 **Meine Mutter hat die Nummer von meinem Handy.**
5 **Meine Ferien waren/mein Urlaub war wunderbar.**
6 **Ich habe viel gesehen und viel gegessen.**
7 **Mein Freund Herr Becker fährt heute nach Hamburg.**
8 **Er kommt morgen mit dem Zug zurück.**
9 **Meine Frau muss nach Amerika fliegen, denn ihre Eltern sind krank/weil ihre Eltern krank sind.**
10 **Ich möchte Weihnachten nach Amerika (fahren), aber mit einem Schiff.**

Let's speak German – fast and fluently

◀ CD2, tr 26

Translate each section and check if it is correct, then cover up the answers and say the three or four sentences as quickly as you can. Try to say each group of sentences in 20 to 30 seconds.

Some of the English is in 'German-speak' to help you.

Don't worry if you're getting the **der, die, das** wrong. Just try to remember some of the model answers where **der, die, das** is correct.

The people in my company do not work a lot.
They write many letters on the computer and always talk on the mobile phone.

Die Leute in meiner Firma arbeiten nicht viel.
Sie schreiben viele Briefe auf dem Computer und sprechen immer auf dem Handy.

I know the Ruhrgebiet and Bavaria very well.
Next year I would like to see the Black Forest.
*I must buy a book on (**über**) Germany.*

Ich kenne das Ruhrgebiet und Bayern sehr gut.
Nächstes Jahr möchte ich den Schwarzwald sehen.
Ich muss ein Buch über Deutschland kaufen.

Hello, what are you doing here? What's the matter?
I need to repair my car and my flat. Both are very old.
The bill is terrible. Can you help me please – with 500 euros?

Hallo, was machen Sie hier? Was ist los?
Ich muss mein Auto und meine Wohnung reparieren. Beide sind sehr alt.
Die Rechnung ist schrecklich. Können Sie mir bitte helfen – mit 500 Euro?

Test your progress

I have put a lot into this last test including all 32 verbs. But don't panic – it looks worse than it is. Go for it – you'll do brilliantly!

Translate into German:

1 I enjoy writing letters because I have a new computer.
2 How are you? What is the matter? Can I help you?
3 How many boring people from the office are coming?
4 I do not have the number of her mobile, I am sorry.
5 I like the Black Forest. We had a lot of snow there last year.
6 The second case is in the bus. Can you take the brown bag?
7 How many cards did you write (at) Christmas?
8 That's crazy: I believe somebody has eaten my steak!
9 Why did you not telephone? We waited until yesterday.
10 Quickly! Have you seen a taxi? My plane is waiting.
11 Don't you know that? The airport is always open – day and night.
12 It is important that you are happy with your holiday.
13 I worked on a boat and was never seasick.
14 Did you see me in the newspaper?... without shoes!
15 Your mother is very nice and makes wonderful apple cake.
16 Do you live in a house or a flat in Germany?
17 We must both work. Three boys and two girls cost a lot of money.
18 We hope the garage can repair that.
19 I know him. He always goes shopping with his dog.
20 Who said one cannot smoke here?
21 We fly to Dallas. Then we take a car and drive to Las Vegas.
22 I would like to speak with the sales assistant. He did not give me a receipt.
23 We drank your wine but we have bought two new bottles.
24 I am sorry, but **Fast German with Elisabeth Smith** is now finished.

Check your answers, then enter a final excellent score on the **Progress chart** and write out your **Certificate**.

Answers

How to score

From a total of 100%:

- Subtract 1% for each wrong or missing word.
- Subtract 1% for wrong form of verb, e.g. **Ich gehen**; **wir hat gekauft**.
- Subtract 1% if you forgot to split the two verbs in a sentence, e.g. **Ich möchte kaufen einen Hund. Ich habe gesehen ein Taxi**.

There are no penalties for:

- Wrong use of: **der, die, das, dem, den, ein, eine, einem, einen, diesem**, etc.
- Wrong ending of word, example: **mit Herr Schmidt; in der gross Tüte**. In a very few cases you will not already have met the correct word ending that you see in the answer. As long as you have the right word, you're doing fine and will be understood. Remember, near enough is good enough.
- Wrong choice of very similar words such as **zu/nach** or **an/bei**.
- Wrong word order, for example: **Morgen wir kommen zurück mit dem Zug** (should be **Wir kommen morgen mit dem Zug zurück**).
- Wrong spelling, as long as you can say the word!

> **100% MINUS YOUR PENALTIES WILL GIVE YOU YOUR WEEKLY SCORE.**

Week 1: Test your progress

1 Mein Name ist Peter Smith.
2 Guten Tag, wir sind Helen und Elke.
3 Ich bin auch aus Hamburg.
4 Ich war im Oktober in Frankfurt.
5 Meine Frau und ich waren drei Jahre in Amerika.
6 Wir fliegen immer im Juni nach Berlin.
7 Wie war Ihr Urlaub in England?
8 Entschuldigen Sie bitte, was machen Sie jetzt in London?
9 Sind Sie Frau Becker aus Bonn?
10 Das Haus in Hannover ist für meine Kinder.
11 Einen Moment bitte, ich habe das Geld.
12 Gibt es hier ein Telefon? Nein, leider nicht.
13 Ich bin ohne meine Frau in England.
14 Wie gross ist Ihre Firma?
15 Kostet ein Mercedes viel Geld?
16 England ist leider nicht schön im Februar.
17 Udo hat eine Freundin im Reisebüro.
18 Der Tag in Holland war langweilig.
19 Mein Job ist sehr gut, aber Urlaub ist besser.
20 Meine zwei Kinder haben viel Geld.

> Your score: _____ %
> Correct those answers that differ from ours.
> Then read them out loud twice.

Week 2: Test your progress

1 Ich trinke viel Bier.
2 Wieviel kostet das Frühstück, bitte?
3 Gibt es ein Reisebüro hier?
4 Haben Sie einen Tisch? In fünfzehn Minuten?
5 Ich möchte etwas trinken.
6 Mein Urlaub in Florida war sehr gut.
7 Wo gibt es eine gute Pension?
8 Kann ich bitte die Rechnung für das Telefon haben?
9 Wir waren nur einmal in Köln.
10 Meine Kinder sind jetzt gross genug.

11 Um wieviel Uhr sind Sie morgen in der Firma?
12 Ich bin immer von halb acht bis Viertel nach fünf da.
13 Eine Frage bitte: wo sind die Toiletten? Geradeaus?
14 Wir möchten im Januar nach Oslo fliegen. Aber es ist zu kalt.
15 Kostet das mehr Geld?
16 Wo sind Sie morgen um halb elf?
17 Es ist schrecklich, es gibt nicht einen Job ohne einen Computer.
18 Können wir hier jetzt essen und haben Sie Platz (or Plätze) für sechs?
19 Wir haben ein kleines Haus in Amerika, aber es war sehr teuer.
20 Auf Wiedersehen, wir fahren jetzt nach Hamburg.

Your score: _____ %

Week 3: Test your progress

1 Können Sie einen Verkäufer sehen?
2 Wo können wir etwas zu essen kaufen?
3 Wann müssen Sie heute in die Firma? Um sieben? Wie schrecklich!
4 Wir haben das gestern im Fernsehen gesehen.
5 Ich glaube, die Geschäfte sind jetzt offen.
6 Gibt es hier ein Kaufhaus oder ein Zentrum mit Geschäften?
7 Entschuldigen Sie, gehen Sie auch zur Post?
8 Wo haben Sie die englische Zeitung gekauft?
9 Wer möchte Wein und wer möchte Bier trinken?
10 Das Wetter ist morgen schlecht. Das ist nicht nett.
11 Das ist alles? Das war billig.
12 Die Briefmarken kosten genau fünf Euro.
13 Der Geldautomat ist für alle Kreditkarten.
14 Sind 300 Gramm Käse zuviel? Nein, kein Problem.
15 Es gibt eine neue Reinigung drei Minuten von hier.
16 Haben Sie bitte eine Tüte für meine Schuhe?
17 Ich glaube, ich habe hier eine Apotheke gesehen.
18 Ach, du meine Güte, alle Eier und drei Flaschen sind kaputt!
19 Können Sie das sehen? Ist das Baumwolle?
20 Grösse zwölf in England – was ist das hier?

Your score: _____ %

Week 4: Test your progress

1 Ich bin sicher, unser Termin war Dienstag.
2 Heute? Nein, das ist nicht möglich. Wir haben leider keine Zeit.
3 Ich muss ein paar Sachen für meine Freunde kaufen.
4 Können Sie mir bitte helfen? Ich möchte die Nummer vom Arzt.
5 Wissen Sie, wo es ein gutes Restaurant gibt?
6 Ich glaube die Kirche ist sehr interessant, aber niemand möchte sie sehen.
7 Wir möchten nächsten Montag abend fliegen.
8 Können Sie mir bitte die Speisekarte geben?
9 Haben Sie ihm Ihre Papiere gegeben?
10 Kann man hier Obst und Gemüse kaufen?
11 Kennen Sie sein neues Buch?
12 Es war wunderbar, vielen Dank für den netten Abend!
13 Warum müssen Sie meine Kreditkarte sehen?
14 Die zwei Wochen auf der QE II waren ein bisschen langweilig.
15 Sie sehen den Geldautomaten oben am Ausgang, bei der Tür.
16 Wir essen Huhn oder Bratwurst – der Fisch ist zu teuer.
17 Wie sagt man auf Deutsch...?
18 Wissen Sie, wo es hier einen Bus gibt?
19 Mein Mann fährt gern nach Texas, aber ich fahre lieber nach Arizona.
20 Sie haben nicht gesagt, wo dieses gemütliche Restaurant war.

Your score: _____ %

Week 5: Test your progress

1 Diese Tasche gefällt mir nicht, die andere Tasche war besser.
2 Wieviel kostet die Fahrkarte – hin und zurück?
3 Was haben Sie gesagt? Können Sie bitte langsam sprechen?
4 Ich weiss, dass Benzin in Amerika billiger ist.
5 Es ist verboten, in der U-Bahn zu rauchen.
6 Ich kann nicht warten. Ich habe einen zweiten Termin um elf Uhr.
7 Ist dieser Kasten für Briefe? Ein gelber Briefkasten?
8 Hallo, wir sind 30 km von Hannover. Ist das die Werkstatt?
9 Was ist schneller: der Zug oder das Auto auf der Autobahn?
10 Est ist diese Woche sehr heiss. Ich möchte lieber ein bisschen Regen.

11 Er hat die Ampel nicht gesehen und jetzt sind sie beide im Krankenhaus.

12 Ich habe sie heute zweimal an der Tankstelle gesehen. Ihr Auto trinkt Benzin!

13 Wo gibt es eine Reinigung? Ich habe Öl auf meinem Armani T-Shirt.

14 Wir wohnen hinter der Hauptstrasse, genau bei/an der Bushaltestelle.

15 Wir sind bei der Polizei, weil unser Handy weg ist/denn unser Handy ist weg.

16 Die Fahrkarten sind billiger, wenn Sie sie jetzt kaufen.

17 Ihr Auto gefällt mir. War es sehr teuer?

18 Können Sie uns bitte helfen? Wo kann man hier am/beim See essen?

Your score: _____ %

Week 6: Say it simply

1 (Entschuldigen Sie), Sie haben mir jetzt ein Auto gegeben. Aber die Farbe ist ein bisschen kaputt. Links, hinter der Tür. Bitte können Sie kommen und es sehen und es auf mein Papier schreiben.

2 Hallo/Guten Tag, ich bin Kate Walker. Ich war in Ihrem Hotel, Zimmer Nr… bis heute. Ich habe leider im Zimmer Sachen von mir und ich bin jetzt im Flughafen. Ich möchte die Sachen bitte nach England. Das Hotel weiss, wo ich wohne. Vielen Dank.

WEEK 6: Spot the keys

1 It depends when you are going. Normally it takes 20 minutes. But if there is a lot of traffic and the Bleichen Bridge is blocked you have to allow three-quarters of an hour. You can read the price on the meter. Normally it is roughly between 10 and 15 euros.

2 They had of course been to… *England*!

WEEK 6: Test your progress

1 Ich schreibe gern Briefe, weil ich einen neuen Computer habe/ denn ich habe einen neuen Computer.

2 Wie geht's? Was ist los? Kann ich Ihnen helfen?

3 Wieviele langweilige Leute von der Firma kommen?

4 Ich habe nicht die Nummer von ihrem Handy. Es tut mir Leid.

5 Der Schwarzwald gefällt mir. Wir hatten da letztes Jahr viel Schnee.

6 Der zweite Koffer ist im Bus. Können Sie die braune Tasche nehmen?

7 Wieviele Karten haben Sie Weihnachten geschrieben?

8 Das ist verrückt: ich glaube jemand hat mein Steak gegessen!

9 Warum haben Sie nicht telefoniert? Wir haben bis gestern gewartet.

10 Schnell! Haben Sie ein Taxi gesehen? Mein Flugzeug wartet.

11 Wissen Sie das nicht? Der Flughafen ist immer offen – Tag und Nacht.

12 Est ist wichtig, dass Sie mit Ihrem Urlaub zufrieden sind.

13 Ich habe auf einem Schiff gearbeitet und war nie seekrank.

14 Haben Sie mich in der Zeitung gesehen?... ohne Schuhe!

15 Ihre Mutter ist sehr nett und macht wunderbaren Apfelkuchen.

16 Wohnen Sie in Deutschland in einem Haus oder in einer Wohnung?

17 Wir müssen beide arbeiten. Drei Jungen und zwei Mädchen kosten viel Geld.

18 Wir hoffen, die Werkstatt kann das reparieren.

19 Ich kenne ihn, er geht immer mit seinem Hund einkaufen.

20 Wer hat gesagt, man kann hier nicht rauchen?

21 Wir fliegen nach Dallas. Dann nehmen wir ein Auto und fahren nach Las Vegas.

22 Ich möchte mit dem Verkäufer sprechen. Er hat mir keine Rechnung gegeben.

23 Wir haben Ihren Wein getrunken, aber wir haben zwei neue Flaschen gekauft.

24 Es tut mir Leid, aber **Fast German with Elisabeth Smith** ist jetzt zuende.

German–English dictionary

In this section you'll find all the **New words** that you have learned, including the 'extras', in alphabetical order.

To make it easy for you to find what you may have forgotten, words are shown exactly as they appear in the **New words** section. For example, if you learned *a few* you'll find it under *'a'*. If you don't remember how to say *I think* you'll find it under *'I'*.

aber but
ach, du meine Güte!
   good grief!
ach so I see
acht eight
achtzehn eighteen
achtzig eighty
alle, alles all
also... well...
alt old
Ampel traffic light
an at
andere, anderer, anderes
   other, other one
Apfelkuchen apple cake
Apotheke chemist's
April April
arbeite/arbeiten am working/
   are working, work
Arzt doctor
auch also
auf on
auf Wiedersehen
   goodbye
August August

aus out of, from
Ausgang exit
Auto car
Autobahn motorway

Bad bath
Bahnhof (railway) station
Baumwolle cotton
bei at
beide both
beim at the
Benzin petrol
besser better
Bier beer
billig cheap
bin am
bis until
bitte please
blau blue
Bratwurst fried sausage
braun brown
Brief letter
Briefmarken stamps
Brot bread
Buch book

Bus bus
Butter butter

Café café

da there
danke thank you
dann then
das the
das (*by itself*) that
das geht nicht that's not on,
　that's not possible
das kostet that costs
dass that
dasselbe the same
dem the
den the
denn because
der the
Deutschland Germany
Dezember December
die the
die Monate months, the
die Toiletten toilets, the
Dienstag Tuesday
dies, dieser, dieses this
Donnerstag Thursday
Doppelzimmer double room
drei three
dreihundert three hundred
dreissig thirty
dreizehn thirteen
dunkel dark
Dusche shower

Ei, Eier egg, eggs
ein a
ein bisschen a little

ein paar a few
eine a
einem a
einen a
einkaufen to do the shopping
einmal once
eins one
Eis ice cream
elf eleven
Eltern parents
Ende end
entschuldigen Sie
　excuse me
er he
Erkältung cold
erste first
es it
es gefällt mir nicht I don't
　like it (it pleases me not)
es gibt (*lit.* it gives) there is,
　there are
es tut mir Leid I'm sorry
essen eat
etwas some, something

fahren drive, travel, go
Fahrkarte ticket
Februar February
Fernsehen television
fertig ready
Firma company, firm, office
Fisch fish
Flasche, Flaschen bottle,
　bottles
Fleisch meat
fliege/fliegen am flying/
　are flying, fly
Flug flight

Flughafen airport
Flugzeug aeroplane
Foto photo
Frage question
Frau Mrs, wife, woman
Freitag Friday
Freundin girlfriend
Friseur hairdresser's
Frühstück breakfast
fünf five
fünfzehn fifteen
fünfzig fifty
für for
Fussball football

geben give
gegeben given
gegessen eaten
gehen go
geholfen helped
gekauft bought
gelb yellow
Geld money
Geldautomat cashpoint
  machine
Gemüse vegetables
gemütlich comfortable, cosy
genau exactly
genommen taken
genug enough
geradeaus straight on
gern gladly, very much
gesagt said
Geschäft, Geschäfte shop,
  shops
gesehen seen
gesprochen spoken
100 **gestern** yesterday

gewartet waited
Glas glass
glauben believe, think
Gleis platform, track
Gramm gram
grau grey
gross, grosse, grosses big
Grösse size
grün green
gut good
gute Nacht good night
guten Abend good evening
guten Morgen good morning
guten Tag good day, hello

habe have
haben have
halb half
halb zehn half past nine
hallo hello
Haltestelle stop
Handy mobile phone
hat has
hatten they had
Hauptstrasse main road
Haus house
heiss hot
helfen help
Herr gentleman, Mr
heute today
hier here
hin und zurück return
  (ticket), there and back
hinter behind
hoffen hope
Huhn chicken
Hund dog
hundert hundred

ich I
ich glaube I believe, I think
ich muss I must
ihm him
ihn him
ihnen them
Ihnen you (*polite*)
ihr her
Ihr your
Ihre your
Ihrem your
Ihren your
im in the
immer always
in in
interessant interesting
ist is

ja yes
Jahr, Jahre year, years
Januar January
Juli July
Juni June

kalt cold
kann can
kaputt broken
Karstadt department store
  (*name of*)
Karte card, map, postcard
Kartoffeln potatoes
Käse cheese
Kasten box
kaufen buy
Kaufhaus department store
kein no
kein Problem no problem
keine no

Kellner waiter
kennen know, to know
Kilometer kilometre
Kinder children
Kirche church
klein small
kleine small
kleines small
Koffer suitcase
kommen come
können can
krank sick
Krankenhaus hospital
Kreditkarte credit card
Kuchen cake
Kunde client

langsam slow, slowly
langweilig boring
leider unfortunately
letzte last
Leute people
lieber rather (*i.e.* prefer)
links left
Liter litre

mache/machen am doing/
  make, do, are doing
Mädchen girl
Mai May
man one
Mann husband, man
März March
mehr more
mein my
meine my
Meter metre
mich me

Milch milk
Minuten minutes
mit with
Mittwoch Wednesday
möchten would like
möglich possible
Moment moment
Monat, ein a month
Montag Monday
morgen tomorrow
Motor engine
müssen must
Mutter mother

nach after, to
nächste woche next week
Nacht night
Nachtisch dessert
Name name
natürlich of course
nehmen take
nein no
nett nice
neu new
neun nine
neunzehn nineteen
neunzig ninety
nicht not
Nichtraucher non-smoker,
  non-smoking (compartment)
nichts nothing
nie never
niemand nobody
November November
Null zero
Nummer, Nummern number,
  numbers

102 nur only

oben at the top, upstairs
Obst fruit
oder or
offen open
oft often
ohne without
Oktober October
Öl oil
Orange orange

Papier paper
Platz place, seat
Polizei police, police station
Post post office

rauchen smoke
Raucher smoker, smoking
  (compartment)
Rechnung bill
rechts right
Regen rain
Reinigung dry cleaner's
Reisebüro travel agency,
  travel office
reparieren (to) repair
richtig right
rosa pink
rot red
Ruhrgebiet industrial area
  of Germany

Sache matter, thing
sagen say
Sahne cream
Salat salad
Samstag Saturday
sauber clean
Schiff ship

schinken ham
schlecht bad
Schmerzen pains
Schnee snow
schnell quick, quickly
schön beautiful, handsome, lovely
schrecklich terrible
schreiben write
Schuhgeschäft shoe shop
Schule sohool
schwarz black
schwer difficult, heavy
sechs six
sechzehn sixteen
sechzig sixty
See lake, sea
sehen see
sehr very
sehr viel very much
sein his
September September
sicher certainly, sure
Sie you (*polite*)
sie she, her
sie hatte she had
sie weiss she knows
sieben seven
siebenhundert seven hundred
siebzehn seventeen
siebzig seventy
sind are
so… wie as… as
Sonnabend Saturday
Sonne sun
Sonntag Sunday
später later

Speisekarte menu
sprechen speak
Stadt city, town
Stück piece
Stunde, eine Stunde hour, an hour
Suppe soup

Tag, Tage day, days
Tankstelle petrol station
Tasche bag
Tasse oup
tausend thousand
Tee tea
Telefon telephone
telefonieren telephone
telefoniert telephones
Termin appointment
teuer expensive
Tisch table
trinken drink
Tür door
Tüte bag (*paper or plastic*)

U-Bahn underground
Uhr clock
um at (*a certain time*)
um…Uhr at…o'clock
um wieviel Uhr? at what time?
und and
uns us
unser, unsere our
(da) unten at the bottom, down (there)
unterwegs on the move
Urlaub holidays

103

verboten forbidden
Verkäufer sales assistant
verrückt crazy
viel a lot of, much
vielen Dank thank you very much
vielleicht perhaps
vier four
viertel quarter
viertel nach quarter past
viertel vor quarter to
vierzehn fourteen
vierzig forty
voll full
von from
vor before

wann when
war was
waren were
warten wait
warum why
was what
was ist los? what is the matter?
Wasser water
weg gone
Weihnachten Christmas
weil because
Wein wine
weiss white
wenn if, when
wer who
Werkstatt garage, workshop
Wetter weather
wichtig important
wie how

wie geht's? how are you?
wie sagt man... auf Deutsch? how do you say... in German?
Wiener Vienna sausages (hot dogs)
wieviel, wieviele how much/many
wir we
wissen know (something)
wo where
Woche, eine a week
wohnen live
Wohnung apartment, flat
Wolle wool
wunderbar wonderful

Zahlen numbers
zehn ten
Zeit time
Zeitung newspaper
Zentrum centre
Zimmer room
zu too, to
Zucker sugar
zuende finished, over
zuerst first
zufrieden content, happy
Zug train
zum to the
zur to the
zuviel too much
zwanzig twenty
zwei two
zweihundert two hundred
zweimal twice
zweite second

English–German dictionary

a **ein, eine, einem, einen**
a few **ein paar**
a little **ein bisschen**
a lot of **viel**
aeroplane **Flugzeug**
after **nach**
airport **Flughafen**
all **alle, alles**
also **auch**
always **Immer**
am **bin**
and **und**
apartment **Wohnung**
apple cake **Apfelkuchen**
appointment **Termin**
April **April**
are **sind**
are doing/am doing **machen/mache**
are flying/am flying **fliegen/fliege**
are working/am working **arbeiten/arbeite**
as… as **so… wie**
at **an, bei**
at (*a certain time*) **um**
at… o'clock **um… Uhr**
at the **beim**
at the bottom **(da) unten**
at the top **oben**

at what time? **um wieviel Uhr?**
August **August**

bad **schlecht**
bag **Tasche**
bag (*paper or plastic*) **Tüte**
bath **Bad**
beautiful **schön**
because **denn, weil**
beer **Bier**
before **vor**
behind **hinter**
believe **glauben**
better **besser**
big **gross, grosse, grosses**
bill **Rechnung**
black **schwarz**
blue **blau**
book **Buch**
boring **langweilig**
both **beide**
bottle, bottles **Flasche, Flaschen**
bought **gekauft**
box **Kasten**
bread **Brot**
breakfast **Frühstück**
broken **kaputt**
brown **braun**
bus **Bus**
but **aber**

butter **Butter**
buy **kaufen**

café **Café**
cake **Kuchen**
can **kann, können**
car **Auto**
card **Karte**
cashpoint machine **Geldautomat**
centre **Zentrum**
certainly **sicher**
cheap **billig**
cheese **Käse**
chemist's **Apotheke**
chicken **Huhn**
children **Kinder**
Christmas **Weihnachten**
church **Kirche**
city **Stadt**
clean **sauber**
client **Kunde**
clock **Uhr**
cold **Erkältung, kalt**
come **kommen**
comfortable **gemütlich**
company **Firma**
content **zufrieden**
cosy **gemütlich**
cotton **Baumwolle**
crazy **verrückt**
cream **Sahne**
credit card **Kreditkarte**
cup **Tasse**

dark **dunkel**
day, days **Tag, Tage**
106 December **Dezember**

department store **Kaufhaus**
department store (*name of*) **Karstadt**
dessert **Nachtisch**
difficult **schwer**
do **machen**
doctor **Arzt**
dog **Hund**
door **Tür**
double room **Doppelzimmer**
down (there) **(da) unten**
drink **trinken**
drive **fahren**
dry cleaner's **Reinigung**

eat **essen**
eaten **gegessen**
egg, eggs **Ei, Eier**
eight **acht**
eighteen **achtzehn**
eighty **achtzig**
eleven **elf**
end **Ende**
engine **Motor**
enough **genug**
exactly **genau**
excuse me **entschuldigen Sie**
exit **Ausgang**
expensive **teuer**

February **Februar**
fifteen **fünfzehn**
fifty **fünfzig**
finished **zuende**
firm **Firma**
first **erste, zuerst**
fish **Fisch**

five **fünf**
flat **Wohnung**
flight **Flug**
fly **fliegen**
football **Fussball**
for **für**
forbidden **verboten**
forty **vierzig**
four **vier**
fourteen **vierzehn**
Friday **Freitag**
fried sausage **Bratwurst**
from **aus, von**
fruit **Obst**
full **voll**

garage **Werkstatt**
gentleman **Herr**
Germany **Deutschland**
girl **Mädchen**
girlfriend **Freundin**
give **geben**
given **gegeben**
gladly **gern**
glass **Glas**
go **fahren, gehen**
gone **weg**
good **gut**
good day **guten Tag**
good evening **guten Abend**
good grief! **ach, du meine Güte!**
good morning **guten Morgen**
good night **gute Nacht**
goodbye **auf Wiedersehen**
gram **Gramm**
green **grün**
grey **grau**

hairdresser's **Friseur**
half **halb**
half past nine **halb zehn**
ham **Schinken**
handsome **schön**
happy **zufrieden**
have/has **haben, habe/hat**
he **er**
heavy **schwer**
hello **guten Tag, hallo**
help **helfen**
helped **geholfen**
her **ihr, sie**
here **hier**
him **ihm, ihn**
his **sein**
holidays **Urlaub**
hope **hoffen**
hospital **Krankenhaus**
hot **heiss**
hour, an hour **Stunde, eine Stunde**
house **Haus**
how **wie**
how are you? **wie geht's?**
how do you say… in German? **wie sagt man… auf Deutsch?**
how much, how many **wieviel, wieviele**
hundred **hundert**
husband **Mann**

I **ich**
I believe **ich glaube**
I don't like it (it pleases me not) **es gefällt mir nicht**
I must **ich muss**

I see **ach so**
I think **ich glaube**
I'm sorry **es tut mir Leid**
ice cream **Eis**
if **wenn**
important **wichtig**
in **in**
in the **im**
industrial area of Germany
   Ruhrgebiet
interesting **interessant**
is **ist**
it **es**

January **Januar**
July **Juli**
June **Juni**

kilometre **Kilometer**
know (something) **wissen**
know, to know **kennen**

lake **See**
last **letzte**
later **später**
left **links**
letter **Brief**
litre **Liter**
live **wohnen**
lovely **schön**

main road **Hauptstrasse**
make **machen**
man **Mann**
map **Karte**
March **März**
matter **Sache**
May **Mai**

me **mich**
meat **Fleisch**
menu **Speisekarte**
metre **Meter**
milk **Milch**
minute, a **eine Minute**
minutes **Minuten**
mobile phone **Handy**
moment **Moment**
Monday **Montag**
money **Geld**
month, a **ein Monat**
months, the **die Monate**
more **mehr**
mother **Mutter**
motorway **Autobahn**
Mr **Herr**
Mrs **Frau**
much **viel**
must **müssen**
my **mein, meine**

name **Name**
never **nie**
new **neu**
newspaper **Zeitung**
next week **nächste Woche**
nice **nett**
night **Nacht**
nine **neun**
nineteen **neunzehn**
ninety **neunzig**
no **kein, keine, nein**
no problem **kein Problem**
nobody **niemand**
non-smoker **Nichtraucher**
non-smoking (compartment)
   Nichtraucher

not **nicht**
nothing **nichts**
November **November**
number, numbers **Nummer, Nummern/Zahlen**

October **Oktober**
of course **natürlich**
office **Firma**
often **oft**
oil **Öl**
old **alt**
on **auf**
on the move **unterwegs**
once **einmal**
one **eins, man**
only **nur**
open **offen**
or **oder**
orange **Orange**
other, other one **anderer, andere, anderes**
our **unser, unsere**
out of **aus**
over **zuende**

pains **Schmerzen**
paper **Papier**
parents **Eltern**
people **Leute**
perhaps **vielleicht**
petrol **Benzin**
petrol station **Tankstelle**
photo **Foto**
piece **Stück**
pink **rosa**
place **Platz**
platform **Gleis**

please **bitte**
police **Polizei**
police station **Polizei**
possible **möglich**
post office **Post**
postcard **Karte**
potatoes **Kartoffeln**

quarter **viertel**
quarter past **viertel nach**
quarter to **viertel vor**
question **Frage**
quick, quickly **schnell**

rain **Regen**
rather (*i.e.* prefer) **lieber**
ready **fertig**
red **rot**
(to) repair **reparieren**
return (ticket) **hin und zurück**
right **rechts, richtig**
room **Zimmer**

said **gesagt**
salad **Salat**
sales assistant **Verkäufer**
Saturday **Sonnabend/ Samstag**
say **sagen**
school **Schule**
sea **See**
seat **Platz**
second **zweite**
see **sehen**
seen **gesehen**
September **September**
seven **sieben**

seven hundred **siebenhundert**
seventeen **siebzehn**
seventy **siebzig**
she **sie**
she had **sie hatte**
she knows **sie weiss**
ship **Schiff**
shoe shop **Schuhgeschäft**
shop, shops **Geschäft, Geschäfte**
shower **Dusche**
sick **krank**
six **sechs**
sixteen **sechzehn**
sixty **sechzig**
size **Grösse**
slow, slowly **langsam**
small **klein, kleine, kleines**
smoke **rauchen**
smoker **Raucher**
smoking (compartment) **Raucher**
snow **Schnee**
some **etwas**
something **etwas**
soup **Suppe**
speak **sprechen**
spoken **gesprochen**
stamps **Briefmarken**
(railway) station **Bahnhof**
stop **Haltestelle**
straight on **geradeaus**
sugar **Zucker**
suitcase **Koffer**
sun **Sonne**
Sunday **Sonntag**
sure **sicher**

table **Tisch**
take **nehmen**
taken **genommen**
tea **Tee**
telephone **Telefon**
telephone/telephones **telefonieren/telefoniert**
television **Fernsehen**
ten **zehn**
terrible **schrecklich**
thank you **danke**
thank you very much **vielen Dank**
that **das** (by itself), **dass**
that costs **das kostet**
that's not on **das geht nicht**
that's not possible **das geht nicht**
the **das, dem, den, der, die**
the same **dasselbe**
them **ihnen**
then **dann**
there **da**
there and back **hin und zurück**
there are **es gibt** (lit. it gives)
there is **es gibt** (lit. it gives)
they had **hatten**
thing **Sache**
think **glauben**
thirteen **dreizehn**
thirty **dreissig**
this **dies, dieser, dieses**
thousand **tausend**
three **drei**
three hundred **dreihundert**
Thursday **Donnerstag**
ticket **Fahrkarte**

time **Zeit**
to **nach, zu**
to do the shopping **einkaufen**
to the **zum, zur**
today **heute**
toilets, the **die Toiletten**
tomorrow **morgen**
too **zu**
too much **zuviel**
town **Stadt**
track **Gleis**
traffic light **Ampel**
train **Zug**
travel **fahren**
travel agency, travel office
   Reisebüro
Tuesday **Dienstag**
twenty **zwanzig**
twice **zweimal**
two **zwei**
two hundred **zweihundert**

underground **U-Bahn**
unfortunately **leider**
until **bis**
upstairs **oben**
us **uns**

vegetables **Gemüse**
very **sehr**
very much **sehr viel, gern**
Vienna sausages (hot dogs)
  Wiener

wait **warten**
waited **gewartet**
waiter **Kellner**

was **war**
water **Wasser**
we **wir**
weather **Wetter**
Wednesday **Mittwoch**
week, a **eine Woche**
well… **also…**
were **waren**
what **was**
what is the matter? **was**
   ist los?
when **wann, wenn**
where **wo**
white **weiss**
who **wer**
why **warum**
wife **Frau**
wine **Wein**
with **mit**
without **ohne**
woman **Frau**
wonderful **wunderbar**
wool **Wolle**
work **arbeiten**
workshop **Werkstatt**
would like **möchten**
write **schreiben**

year, a **ein Jahr**
year, years **Jahr, Jahre**
yellow **gelb**
yes **ja**
yesterday **gestern**
you *(polite)* **Sie, Ihnen**
your **Ihr, Ihre, Ihrem, Ihren**

zero **Null**

How to use the flash cards

Learning words and sentences can be tedious but with **flash cards** it's quick and good fun.

This is what you do

When the **Day-by-day guide** tells you to use the cards cut them out, photocopy them or copy them on to card. There are **Flash words** and **Flash sentences** for each week. Each card has a little number on it telling you to which week it belongs, so you won't cut out too many cards at a time or muddle them up later on.

First, try to learn the words and sentences by looking at both sides. Then, when you have a rough idea, start testing yourself – that's the fun bit. Look at the English, say the German and then check. Make a pile for the 'correct' ones and one for the 'wrong' and 'don't know' ones. When all the cards are used up start again with the 'wrong' pile and try to whittle it down until you get all of them right. You can also play it 'backwards' by starting with the German face up.

Take them the cards with you on the bus, the train, to the hairdresser's or the dentist's. Do a quick 'turn and learn' whenever you have a bit of spare time.

The **Flash words** for each week are there to start you off. Convert the rest of the **New words** into **Flash cards**, too.

It's well worth it!

Flash cards for 'fast' learning:
Don't lose them – use them!

Flugzeug 1	**sind** 1
bin 1	**nach** 1
Sie 1	**auch** 1
aber 1	**sehr** 1
arbeiten 1	**jetzt** 1
leider 1	**wie** 1

Cut out and use ✂

are [1]	aeroplane [1]
to, after [1]	am [1]
also [1]	you [1]
very [1]	but [1]
now [1]	work [1]
how [1]	unfortunately [1]

Cut out and use ✂

Ihr, Ihre <div align="right">1</div>	**langweilig** <div align="right">1</div>
immer <div align="right">1</div>	**viel** <div align="right">1</div>
Urlaub <div align="right">1</div>	**ohne** <div align="right">1</div>
Platz <div align="right">1</div>	**aus** <div align="right">1</div>
Stadt <div align="right">1</div>	**Handy** <div align="right">1</div>
Zimmer <div align="right">2</div>	**teuer** <div align="right">2</div>

Cut out and use ✂

boring ¹	your ¹
much, a lot ¹	always ¹
without ¹	holidays ¹
from, out of ¹	place, seat ¹
mobile phone ¹	town, city ¹
expensive ²	room ²

Cut out and use ✂

2 **vielleicht**	2 **möchten**
2 **genug**	2 **ein bisschen**
2 **schlecht**	2 **wieviel**
2 **nur**	2 **kein, keine**
2 **Frühstück**	2 **von... bis**
2 **fahren**	2 **man**

Cut out and use ✂

would like 2

perhaps 2

a little 2

enough 2

how much, how many 2

bad 2

no 2

only 2

from... to 2

breakfast 2

one 2

go, drive 2

Cut out and use ✂

2	2
geradeaus	**etwas**
2	2
schrecklich	**Rechnung**
2	2
Nacht	**mit**
2	2
Tasse	**oder**
3	3
gehen	**müssen**
3	3
heute	**zu, zum, zur**

Cut out and use ✂

2	2
something	**straight on**
bill	**terrible**
with	**night**
or	**cup**
must	**go**
to	**today**

Cut out and use ✂

3	3
zuerst	**kaufen/ gekauft**
3	3
Geschäft	**gestern**
3	3
wann	**sehen/ gesehen**
3	3
Verkäufer	**wer**
3	3
glauben	**später**
3	3
Stück	**sagen/gesagt**

Cut out and use ✂

buy/bought 3	first 3
yesterday 3	shop, business 3
see/seen 3	when 3
who 3	sales assistant 3
later 3	believe 3
say/said 3	piece 3

Cut out and use ✂

dasselbe 3	**mich** 3
Flasche 3	**Geldautomat** 3
neu 3	**billig** 3
jemand 4	**warum** 4
Termin 4	**wichtig** 4
Sache 4	**möglich** 4

Cut out and use ✂

me 3	**the same** 3
cashpoint machine 3	**bottle** 3
cheap 3	**new** 3
why 4	**someone** 4
important 4	**appointment** 4
possible 4	**thing, matter** 4

Cut out and use ✂

nächste Woche 4	**ach so!** 4
oben 4	**wissen/ gewusst** 4
fertig 4	**Ausgang** 4
ihn, ihm 4	**sicher** 4
natürlich 4	**hinter** 4
geben/ gegeben 4	**niemand** 4

Cut out and use ✂

4 **I see!**	4 **next week**
4 **know/known**	4 **at the top, upstairs**
4 **exit**	4 **ready**
4 **sure**	4 **him**
4 **behind**	4 **of course**
4 **nobody**	4 **give/given**

Cut out and use ✂

4 **unser**	4 **ein paar**
4 **krank**	4 **Speisekarte**
5 **hin und zurück**	5 **Fahrkarte**
5 **Zug**	5 **sprechen/ gesprochen**
5 **warten/ gewartet**	5 **beide**
5 **nehmen/ genommen**	5 **dass**

Cut out and use ✂

a few [4]	**our** [4]
menu [4]	**ill** [4]
ticket [5]	**there and back, return (ticket)** [5]
speak/spoken [5]	**train** [5]
both [5]	**wait/waited** [5]
that [5]	**take/taken** [5]

Cut out and use ✂

5	5
weg	**weil, denn**
5	5
zufrieden	**Hauptstrasse**
5	5
Haltestelle	**Kasten**
5	5
Tankstelle	**Benzin**
5	5
zweimal	**Werkstatt**
5	5
hoffen	**alt**

Cut out and use

because 5	**gone** 5
main road 5	**content, happy** 5
box 5	**stop** 5
petrol 5	**petrol station** 5
workshop, garage 5	**twice** 5
old 5	**hope** 5

Cut out and use ✂

5 **Tasche**	5 **schnell**
5 **heiss**	5 **Regen**
6 **Leute**	6 **ihnen**
6 **Weihnachten**	6 **zuende**
6 **ihr**	6 **nichts**
6 **richtig**	6 **wohnen**

Cut out and use ✂

5	5
quick, quickly	**bag**

5	5
rain	**hot**

6	6
them	**people**

6	6
finished, over	**Christmas**

6	6
nothing	**her**

6	6
live	**right**

Cut out and use ✂

6	6
sie hatte/ hatten	**sein**
6	6
Wohnung	**nie**
6	6
Flughafen	**Mutter**
6	6
Schnee	**Junge**
6	6
Mädchen	**schreiben**
6	6
Schiff	**Flug**

Cut out and use ✂

6	6
his	**she had/had**
6	6
never	**apartment, flat**
6	6
mother	**airport**
6	6
boy	**snow**
6	6
write	**girl**
6	6
flight	**ship, boat**

Cut out and use ✂

Wir waren im Mai in Berlin. 1

für meine Firma 1

Entschuldigen Sie, bitte. 1

Ich arbeite bei Rover. 1

Wir haben jetzt Urlaub. 1

Sind Sie aus London? 1

Wir sind aus Manchester. 1

Ich war bei Shell. 1

Sie hat eine Freundin. 1

Wir fliegen nach Mallorca. 1

Cut out and use

We were in Berlin in May. 1

for my firm 1

Excuse me, please. 1

I work at Rover. 1

We are now on holiday. 1

Are you from London? 1

We are from Manchester. 1

I was at Shell. 1

She has a friend. 1

We fly to Mallorca. 1

Cut out and use

Flash cards

Haben Sie ein Zimmer? 2

Es ist kaputt. 2

Wieviel kostet es? 2

Von acht bis halb zehn. 2

Das ist zu teuer! 2

Wir möchten nach Berlin fahren. 2

Wir möchten etwas essen. 2

Wo gibt es hier...? 2

Wo ist das Café? 2

Um wieviel Uhr? 2

Cut out and use

137

Do you have a room? 2

It is broken. 2

How much does it cost? 2

From eight to half past nine. 2

That is too expensive! 2

We would like to go to Berlin. 2

We would like to eat something. 2

Where is there... here? 2

Where is the café? 2

At what time? 2

Cut out and use

Wir gehen heute einkaufen. 3

Wo gibt es einen Bus? 3

Es tut mir Leid. 3

Wir müssen zuerst zur Bank. 3

Ich möchte Schuhe kaufen. 3

Das ist alles. 3

Wo gibt es hier einen Supermarkt? 3

Wann sind die Geschäfte offen? 3

Wir haben viel gekauft. 3

Ich habe bei Karstadt gegessen. 3

Cut out and use

We are going shopping today. 3

Where is there a bus? 3

I am sorry. 3

First we must (go) to the bank. 3

I would like to buy shoes. 3

That is all. 3

Where is there a supermarket here? 3

When are the shops open? 3

We bought a lot. 3

I have eaten at Karstadt. 3

Cut out and use

Jemand hat telefoniert. 4

Er hat nicht gesagt, warum. 4

Ich habe einen Termin mit ihm. 4

Ich kenne ihn. 4

Das geht nicht. 4

Können Sie mir das geben? 4

Können Sie mir helfen? 4

Essen Sie gern Bratwurst? 4

Ich trinke lieber Wein. 4

Wie sagt man... auf Deutsch? 4

Cut out and use ✂

Someone has phoned. 4

He did not say why. 4

I have an appointment with him. 4

I know him. 4

That's not on. 4

Can you give me that? 4

Can you help me? 4

Do you like eating Bratwurst? 4

I prefer drinking wine. 4

How do you say in German...? 4

Cut out and use ✂

Wo ist der Bahnhof? 5

Wann fährt der Zug? 5

Wie kommen wir zur Autobahn? 5

Wohin fährt dieser Bus? 5

Gibt es hier eine Werkstatt? 5

Wir nehmen das andere. 5

Es gefällt mir nicht. 5

Es war billig, weil es alt ist. 5

Die Tasche ist weg. 5

Ich hoffe, dass Sie ein Auto haben. 5

Cut out and use

Where is the station? 5

When does the train go? 5

How do we get to the motorway? 5

Where (to) does this bus go? 5

Is there a garage here? 5

We'll take the other one. 5

I don't like it. 5

It was cheap because it is old. 5

The bag has gone. 5

I hope that you have a car. 5

Cut out and use ✂

Nächste Woche muss ich arbeiten. 6

Ich kann nicht warten. 6

Wo wohnen Sie? 6

Ich muss mit ihm sprechen. 6

Wir haben eine Dreizimmerwohnung. 6

Unser Urlaub ist jetzt zuende. 6

Was ist los? 6

Wir haben zwei Tage gewartet. 6

Haben Sie das gesehen? 6

Wie geht's? 6

Cut out and use

Next week I must work. 6

I cannot wait. 6

Where do you live? 6

I must speak with him. 6

We have a three-room flat. 6

Our holiday is now over. 6

What is the matter? 6

We waited (for) two days. 6

Did you see that? 6

How is it going?/
How are you? 6

Cut out and use ✂

This is to certify
that

. . . .

has successfully completed
a six-week course of

Fast German
with Elisabeth Smith

with

. . . .

results

Date . . . .

Author ~~Elizabeth Smith~~

Praise for Elisabeth Smith

'A language lifeline ... fun, fast and easy.'
(*The Independent*)

'The simple scripts and audio make it crystal clear ... I'm delighted with my progress.'
(*Greece* magazine)

'Its narration is laid-back and encouraging and the method is straightforward. (4-star review).'
(*Time Out*)

'The elements are simple and very straightforward ... strong encouragement ... plenty of opportunity for spoken practice. This course worked very well for me.'
(*Professional Manager* magazine)

'We think it is wonderful.'
(Tom and Maureen Peil, Preston)

'I loved the sense of humour ... Each week I did the final test with bated breath wondering if this time the little bar chart [...] would take a nose dive – but it didn't.'
(Lesly Hopkins, Twickenham)

'This isn't just a package that asks you remember the names for things in a different language this is a package that teaches ... Highly recommended.'
(Maximus)

'It really is an effective way to learn.'
(Mr R. Ellor)

'A solid product offering excellent value for money ... a great place to start.'
(A. M. Boughey)

'One of the best courses around to get you that little bit further than the basics.'
(Johannsen Krister)

more...

'The words are very clearly spoken and the form of presentation witty and lively to keep your interest, and clever choice of subject matter also keep learning interesting and aid memory. This is a very strong language course and I recommend it.'
(vh1967)

'The Elisabeth Smith courses are a superb resource for the learner who needs to be able to speak the language in a short period of time and with a good degree of understanding.'
(Will Boyce)

'I was surprised at what I'd achieved after this course and recommend it.'

'This is an absolute must have … You'll be so glad you bought it!'
(Elodie)

Now join me on:

Facebook at www.facebook.com/elisabethsmithlanguages

Twitter at www.twitter.com/LanguagesESmith